BEYOND THE JOB DESCRIPTION

How Managers and Employees Can Navigate the True Demands of the Job

JESSE SOSTRIN

Dedication

For Joy: thank you for your enduring belief in
what matters to me.

BEYOND THE JOB DESCRIPTION
Copyright © Jesse Sostrin, 2013.

First published in 2013 by
PALGRAVE MACMILLAN®
in the United States—a division of St. Martin's Press LLC,
175 Fifth Avenue, New York, NY 10010.

Where this book is distributed in the UK, Europe and the rest of the world,
this is by Palgrave Macmillan, a division of Macmillan Publishers Limited,
registered in England, company number 785998, of Houndmills,
Basingstoke, Hampshire RG21 6XS.

Palgrave Macmillan is the global academic imprint of the above companies
and has companies and representatives throughout the world.

Palgrave® and Macmillan® are registered trademarks in the United States,
the United Kingdom, Europe and other countries.

ISBN: 978–1–137–33740–5

Library of Congress Cataloging-in-Publication Data

Sostrin, Jesse.
    Beyond the job description : How Managers and Employees Can
  Navigate the True Demands of the Job / Jesse Sostrin.
      pages cm
    Includes bibliographical references.
    ISBN 978–1–137–33740–5 (alk. paper)
      1. Success in business. 2. Performance. 3. Organizational culture. I. Title.

HF5386.S747 2013
650.1—dc23   2013019912

A catalogue record of the book is available from the British Library.

Design by Newgen Knowledge Works (P) Ltd., Chennai, India.

First edition: December 2013

10 9 8 7 6 5 4 3 2 1

Printed in the United States of America.

CONTENTS

Part 5 Establishing Future-Proof Leaders, Teams, and Organizations

FIGURES AND TABLES

FIGURES

TABLES

PREFACE

BEYOND THE JOB DESCRIPTION IS a book I wish I had when I was learning how to manage people, lead organizations, and coach others to do the same. As a new manager, I found that for every moment of insight and success there were two challenges around every corner. The progress made on one front was just as quickly eroded by another unseen obstacle elsewhere. Constant change from the world outside, combined with the unpredictability of people and circumstances inside the organization, kept me chasing the ghosts of issues that affected my team's performance, my own contributions to the organization, and the bottom line.

Slowly but surely, and with the accumulation of the battle scars to prove it, I discovered the fundamental cause of my greatest challenges in the world of work: *there is a hidden side of work that is constantly felt, but seldom seen.* Whether my focus was on my own responsibilities, managing my team's performance, or leading changes to improve the overall effectiveness of the organization, these *hidden challenges of work* were always there, silently undermining success at every turn.

Despite the endless stream of conventional solutions available to address workplace issues, I realized that something different was needed. There was not even a language to describe the true demands of work that I discovered, let alone tools and reliable resources to address them. Half-hearted responses that failed to get at the root cause of the issue at hand only increased frustration and sustained the damage over time. Recognizing this gap in resources inspired me to build my own set of tools and practices to expose the hidden side of work and effectively address its many challenges.

For over a decade now I have been a cartographer of sorts, painstakingly mapping the ecology and terrain of work's greatest challenges and helping leaders and their organizations to work differently in response to it. I put all of these insights and practices together so that others could decode their greatest challenges at work, and *Beyond the Job Description* is the result.

I stumbled toward my own epiphany about the hidden path to success at work; in contrast, *Beyond the Job Description* provides a roadmap to help you avoid hazardous pitfalls and unforeseen obstacles that threaten your success on the job. Writing the book was a labor of love for me. My hope is that reading it will help you love the results of your labor and lead you toward the working life you want.

JESSE SOSTRIN,

April 2013

ACKNOWLEDGMENTS

I WOULD LIKE TO THANK my late teacher and friend, Charlie Seashore, who thought the world needed more *Jesse*.

I would like to thank my editor, Laurie Harting, for spotting the value in these pages and trusting in me to deliver. And, I would like to thank my editorial assistant, Lauren LoPinto, for making the process of getting this book out to the world easier.

And, finally, I would like to thank the greatest contributors to this book: the countless clients and colleagues I have worked with over the years who trusted me to help them identify and resolve their greatest challenges on the job.

INTRODUCTION

WORK IS THE INESCAPABLE OBLIGATION that defines our lives. However, it isn't the organization we work for or the position we hold; what defines us is *how* we work. Whether you are an individual contributor, a manager, or the leader of an entire organization, you have to work well. Your current performance depends on it. Your access to better assignments and future advancement depend on it. And your quality of life depends on it.

With careers that span more than six decades, it is an unmistakable truth that our lives are "working lives," and the ability to work well is the scaffolding for a long, healthy, and successful life.

However, anybody who has spent five minutes in the workplace knows that there is nothing easy about succeeding at work and that there are no shortcuts to reaching one's full potential. And although the world of work has always evolved, solutions to the challenges of getting great work done are increasingly elusive. The economic stress of the last decade has only intensified the pressure. Retirement is delayed for most people, if it happens at all. The hyper-competitive job market leaves most people looking over their shoulders, wondering whether someone younger, smarter, and more talented is right behind them. And challenges from the inverse equation of *increasing demands* and *shrinking resources* are matched only by the demands of constant change and mounting complexity. For many people, this is the age of uncertainty in the world of work.

"Seventy-one percent of American workers are 'not engaged' or 'actively disengaged' in their work, meaning they are emotionally disconnected from their workplaces and are less likely to be productive."[1]

What are the cumulative effects of this tumultuous environment? For far too many people, surviving is the new thriving at work. This fundamental shift has resulted in chronic disengagement for so many who are overworked and overmatched by the challenges of meeting the full measure of their shifting responsibilities.

Of course, there has been no shortage of resources offered up as solutions to address these workplace challenges. Whether targeted at leaders or individuals, these "new ideas" for reengaging and achieving better results at work reflect the conventional wisdom about what it means to work well. Unfortunately, the conventional wisdom has failed us.

Beyond the Job Description reveals the *hidden curriculum of work*®— it provides a complete picture of the true demands of work and identifies the crucial success factors required for individuals, managers, and leaders to work well in an uncertain world.[2]

By introducing the ground-breaking concept of the "job-within-the-job" and by highlighting the related effects from the "hidden side of work," *Beyond the Job Description* challenges the conventional wisdom about what is required to succeed in today's fast-changing world of work. Working well requires a focus on creating value, solving the problems that reduce learning and performance, and doing these things in a way that merges individual contributions with team and organizational goals. Six questions are presented to help you define your purpose, value-added contributions, and hidden challenges. The result is the first glimpse of your hidden curriculum of work up close. Next, a straightforward and easy-to-use set of tools is introduced to help you identify your core barriers and transform them into opportunities to boost learning and performance. The system is easy to understand and flexible enough to meet the specific needs of managers and employees.

The process is guided by the *R-I-T-E Model*, which includes four progressive stages that allow you to: **R**eveal Your Hidden Curriculum of Work; **I**dentify Barriers That Mark Pathways to Learning and Performance; **T**ransform Barriers and Navigate Your Hidden Path to Success at Work; and **E**stablish Future-Proof Plans for Yourself, Your Team, and Your Organization.

With a mix of related insights, guided coaching activities, and hands-on exercises, the R-I-T-E Model offers a reorientation to the true demands of work and delivers a lifeline for people who need to stand out, stay ahead of the change curve, and navigate the everyday challenges to getting great work done.

Beyond the Job Description will help you uncover your hidden path to success at work. This includes convenient tools for dealing with the everyday challenges that prevent your best work, as well as a complete system for creating a Future-Proof plan that will help you craft the working life you want.

Together, the concepts and tools discussed here offer you a way to align your purpose with team and organizational goals, conduct a real-time analysis of your performance gaps, and show the true value of what you deliver to your team and organization on a consistent basis. If you are starting from scratch, *Beyond the Job Description can* be the centerpiece of your professional and leadership development efforts. If you are engaged in a process now, it will seamlessly blend with your existing commitments to learning, development, and performance improvement.

This is one of those rare business books that not only lays out a research-based argument for why we need a new approach to work, but also delivers a comprehensive set of solutions that readers can absorb and implement immediately.

Are you getting great work done, or are some of your best efforts undermined by unexpected challenges? Are you staying on purpose and delivering added value to your organization, or do you find yourself struggling to make a positive contribution and stay relevant at work? Are you managing and leading in a way that brings others to their maximum contribution, or does your influence fail to make others better and impact the organization's culture and bottom line in positive way? These are unavoidable questions that must be confronted. *Beyond the Job Description will* lead you through an accelerated process to help you find your answers to these and other questions along your path to success at work.

THE MUTUAL AGENDA: BREAKTHROUGHS FOR INDIVIDUALS = SUCCESS FOR ORGANIZATIONS

This is a book about making something better with your experience at work. It is about *working* well and it is about *managing* and *leading* well. If you want to manage others and lead well, you have to work well yourself. If you learn how to work well yourself, then you will likely create opportunities to lead teams and organizations. Wherever you are on the continuum of your career progression—whether you are the CEO of a Fortune 500 company or just the CEO of your own working life—the bottom line is that *your impact* comes from your capacity to perform well over time.

From an individual perspective, this means understanding the true demands of your work and developing the tools to effectively respond to those challenges. From an organizational perspective it means leading change in organizations and creating cultures that are responsive to the hidden challenges of work that undermine priorities and goals. However, distinguishing between individual and organizational perspectives is somewhat distracting.

In reality, you cannot have an organizational perspective without individuals, and the role of individuals is to align their contribution with the intended purpose of the organization. Likewise, you ultimately cannot have success or failure in one without the other. This means that organizational leaders have no choice but to acknowledge that investments that help their people understand the true demands of their work and develop the tools to effectively respond to those challenges is an investment in the organization's overall success. Likewise, individuals have no choice but to reconcile their own career aspirations and desired contributions in the world of work with the specific team and organizational goals they can directly support.

It sounds simple, but there are a few problems with this. The first problem is that the team and the organization do not always know what they want or need from individuals. The position that you were hired to fill and the job description that both sets the trajectory for your overall role and provides you with day-to-day direction for your responsibilities may not reflect what is most needed or valued. The individual impact of this is exacerbated when things change rapidly and the inertia of your ongoing contributions may become irrelevant before they have even been fully realized.

The other problem is that organizations have, by and large, abandoned support for individual professional development. While there are many outstanding exceptions to this unfortunate trend, the reality is that most people must chart a course for their own personal growth and career development. This can often lead to a free-agent mentality that creates inadvertent, unnecessary, and potentially destructive competition between the individual's needs and the organization's needs. You can see this play out in the words of these conflicted professionals:

"I know that I could do more here. I can see our inefficiencies and ways to inno- vate, but I honestly don't know if it is worth fighting to fix because of all the cut- backs lately. We always talk about recruiting people who 'go above and beyond' and yet we don't really have a culture where people can see why they should be motivated to do so." —Middle manager at a midmarket retail company

"I told my manager that I wanted to grow and that I would participate in the leadership development program that our company offers. She told me that the company stopped offering that program last year due to budget cuts and that it would likely not be coming back anytime soon." —Associate at a software devel- opment company

"We just finished a project that literally took six months of my time and lots of blood, sweat, and tears. The day I called my boss to tell him that we were ready to present the results, he said unapologetically that a decision was made to move in another direction. I argued that we potentially had something special with this project, but he flatly said he was sorry 'things just change fast around here.'" —Project manager at an engineering firm

People holding back their good ideas and potential contributions as they wonder if their jobs will evaporate overnight...Future leaders willing to do what it takes to grow, but told to sit tight indefinitely...And, hard workers doing everything they are asked and then told that the work they produce is not needed. A central theme in this book, and a solution to these problems, is discovering the *mutual agenda* where individual goals and team/organization needs intersect.

The *mutual agenda* defines the powerful space where individual goals and desired contributions intersect with organizational objectives. Whether you are an individual contributor, manager, or senior leader, there is a mutual agenda where your own aspirations for your career and the qual- ity of working life you seek will align with the specific needs of your team and organization.

It is not the length of time one spends in a specific job with a particular company; it is the quality of their contribution during that time. Employees can maximize their investment of time in an organization by defining and pursuing their own long-term career goals while staying true to their team and organization's needs. Likewise, managers and leaders can maximize their contributions by clearly defining their team and organizational objectives in a way that accommodates individual hopes and goals.

When there is a severe mismatch between objectives and no clear mutual agenda, employees often quit (and forget to inform their manager), or they take their valued contributions where they can flourish elsewhere. When there is alignment and a clearly accepted mutual agenda, momentum from this synergy can be the counterbalance to complacency and performance gaps among individuals and failed strategies and misaligned team efforts for organizations. It is in this middle ground where breakthrough performance can happen.

THE FLOW OF THE BOOK

Beyond the Job Description unfolds one level at a time, and each successive layer is tightly packed, adding new levels of related knowledge, skills, and capabilities to reveal your hidden curriculum of work. The book is organized in five parts.

Part 1 exposes the true demands of work and lays out the case for a new approach. It confronts the myth of our working lives and reveals the fact that we are all actually working two jobs, whether we know it or not. By contrasting both the "presenting side of work" and the "hidden side of work," it sets the stage for what individuals and teams can do to get ahead of constant change and deal with the inverse equation of increasing demands and decreasing resources.

Part 2 offers a hands-on process to reveal your "job-within-the-job," which includes your vital purpose, value-added contributions, and the hidden challenges that threaten your success at work. Discovering your "job-within-the-job" is the first step toward taking back your working life from the uncertainty of today's hypercompetitive job market and the down economy.

Part 3 introduces a process to translate the everyday obstacles you experience on the job into opportunities to boost your learning and performance. Rather than following the typical response patterns that drain energy and resources, you will learn how to tap barriers for their teachable moments and actually make them work for you. Like a master class on issue resolution, these chapters introduce four essential questions that transform barriers, including: What is the root cause of my challenge? How can I see it from various perspectives to get the full picture? What underlying pattern holds the unwanted experience and outcomes in place? And, what action can I take to resolve this challenge? In order to answer these questions and fully reveal the character and complexity of the hidden side of work, you will learn how to make data-rich visual depictions of performance barriers that objectively clarify your challenges and goals.

After parts 2 and 3 get you on your unique path to success on the job, part 4 provides a variety of inspiring concepts and tools to help you stay on the path to success. It provides a daily compass for solo navigation that will facilitate your first 90 days of implementing the concepts and tools discussed in this book. It responds to realistic concerns about available time and energy to invest in your working life when your plate is already full. And it delivers an unequivocal response to the growing epidemic of a workforce that now includes a majority of people working in a state of disengagement.

Finally, part 5 offers knowledge and practice guides to help you establish future-proof leaders and organizational cultures. With a guide to team navigation, a handbook for managing the hidden side of work, and a groundbreaking set of definitions and insights about the role of leaders and the process of culture change, the related tools and strategies offer an application of the book's concepts and practices to the entire enterprise.

At the conclusion of each chapter there is a summary of Key Takeaways, and at the conclusion of the book there is a set of appendices that offer a variety of assessments and additional resources to further deepen and sustain the application of the book's insights and tools for going *beyond the job description.*

THE BOTTOM LINE

To avoid all of the performance challenges that can derail our success at work we have to find all the holes in our hidden curriculum of work. However, even one crack in our resistance to barriers can undermine our achievements. This fact makes the discipline of navigating the hidden curriculum of work an urgent demand for everyone. By matching this sense of urgency with essential skills to increase individual, team, and organizational performance, *Beyond the Job Description* will increase your capacity to:

- Discover the mutual agenda where your individual values and aspirations align with the needs of your team and the goals of your organization;
- Know what is most important right now and focus on the vital purpose and value-added contributions that can help you stand out and stay ahead of the change curve;

- Establish a system to identify hidden challenges that undermine your performance and learn to transform those barriers into opportunities for improved learning and performance;
- Develop a clear vision and plan to achieve the working life you want;
- Create relationships and preferred patterns of communication and interaction that help you get your best work done, get collaborative decision making right, and make sense of complexity and ambiguity; and
- Learn simple ways to keep people engaged and on the same page during periods of intense change, increase levels of workplace trust and engagement, and change your organization's culture from within.

USE THIS BOOK TO DISCOVER YOUR PATH

The insights and tools in this book are versatile and can be used in a wide range of workplace circumstances. For time-starved and resource-strapped professionals who discern between substantive resources and the revolving "flavor-of-the-month" sound bytes that sound good but offer no useful treatment of the real issues, *Beyond the Job Description provides* a rigorous challenge. While there is real work to be done by the reader, the incisive concepts and useful practices presented in this book will benefit anyone with a stake in their own career success or the success of others. It offers the following advantages:

- *Individual contributors* will learn how to open greater opportunities for advancement by revealing the hidden curriculum of work and turning obstacles into opportunities that boost learning and performance. If you are an individual contributor, you will be able to:
  - o Assess your "job-within-the-job" to gauge the true challenges of your work;
  - o Implement an innovative process of professional development and growth;
  - o Demonstrate increased learning and performance to your direct manager;
  - o Advocate for better assignments that are consistent with your purpose and values;
  - o Communicate clear evidence of your ongoing contributions to the team; and

Chapter 1

THE MYTH OF YOUR WORKING LIFE

YOUR ENTIRE WORKING LIFE IS based on a myth. It all began when you arrived for your first job interview. After you answered a few questions about your background and experience, the interviewer likely gave you *a single job description* that described the tasks and functions required by the role you would fill in the organization. When you were hired you *got the job* and the title to match it. Any training and orientation you received followed that position description, and you were given tools to help you carry out the functions of the job effectively. As you were introduced to new colleagues, you told them the *name of your position* and then described a few of the most prominent tasks in your new role. Likewise, when you asked team members what they did, you heard the same superficial rundown: title, function, and a few basic tasks. From that point on, the myth was firmly set in place. All of the expectations about your contribution to the organization were based on *your job description, title*, and the *day-to-day tasks and activities* they required.

This sequence of events describes the typical experience that the vast majority of people in the world of work live through every day. However, if you have spent even five minutes on the job, you know that something is wrong with this picture. What the team and organization need from you does not always match what your job description says. *The tasks and activities you are responsible for completing are often not the most important things you could be doing.* And, actually fulfilling your responsibilities can be much harder than it looks due to the everyday obstacles that emerge as you work with people and navigate through the unexpected challenges of your day.

The reason that *the expectations you have about work* do not match your *actual experience at work* is because your working life is based on a fundamental misunderstanding of the true demands of work. Many of the common challenges we face at work stem from what Kingsley Davis, the internationally recognized sociologist, called the *double reality*.[1] There is always a double reality: on the one hand, there is a complete system of attitudes and beliefs about *what ought to be* and what *should* happen in a given circumstance based on our expectations. On the other hand, there is the factual order of *what is*. These two realities are not identical, but neither are they ever really separate. The constant tension between our beliefs about *how things should be, what people ought to do and say*, and *how the world should behave* confounds us time and again when these beliefs simply do not conform. Applying this concept to the world of work, we can see how the gap between *our expectations about work* and *our actual experience with work* sustains this double reality and the frustrating contradictions it brings.

Nobody told you this, but the day you were hired you actually accepted two jobs. The first was the position you interviewed for, including the title and all of the tasks and activities outlined in that job description. The second "job-within-the-job" included the unspoken, unwritten work that, among other challenges, requires you to manage constant change, effectively collaborate with others, navigate confusing workplace politics, and get your best work done with a perpetual shortage of time and resources.

Nobody trained you to succeed in this hidden work, and by and large you have been left alone to confront the everyday pitfalls it brings. If working both of these difficult jobs was not hard enough already, staying relevant at work in today's hypercompetitive job market requires you to get ahead of the change curve by steadily *increasing your skills and abilities* and finding innovative ways to *go beyond your primary job description* in order to *add increasing value to your organization.*

These two elements combined—the challenges of your "job-within-the-job" plus the need to add value to your organization through continuous learning and performance—represent what I call the *hidden curriculum of work*.[2] If your current job could be outsourced, downsized, or automated and if you worry that someone else younger, smarter, and hungrier is right behind you, then your best chance of staying relevant in your career is to learn how to navigate your hidden curriculum of work. Learning how to reveal this hidden side of work and gaining the confidence and know-how to meet its everyday challenges will make you *Future-Proof* and give you the best chance for a long, successful working life.

Future-Proof – noun/1: learning to see your hidden curriculum of work, spotting the specific barriers that it produces, and transforming those everyday challenges into opportunities for improved learning and performance; 2: using your continuous learning and performance to stay ahead of the change curve, remain relevant in your career, and craft a meaningful working life.

The implications of the hidden curriculum of work are significant. Every year when you sit down with your manager to receive performance feedback about what you accomplished or failed to achieve, it is based on what your job description says you were supposed to do in that time frame. Your raise, your promotion, and your opportunities to grow in the organization are all tied to these limited, unrealistic expectations about your role, the challenges you actually face, and the most valued contributions you make at work.

While performance appraisals and promotions are the trajectory-setting experiences that shape the long-term arc of a career, the double reality of work also has immediate impacts on the quality of your working life. Learning that the job we were hired to fill is not the only one we're working can be stressful and confusing. Being held accountable for things we are not fully aware of and may not wholly be in our control can be frustrating and demoralizing. And, as the ground underneath you moves at the quickening pace of change, constantly reinventing your own work to accomplish elusive priorities can be both exhilarating and exhausting.

Despite these challenges, this is where things get really interesting. If you can expose your hidden curriculum of work and learn to get past the challenges of its double reality, then you potentially gain powerful leverage to shape the quality of your working life and the outcomes you achieve. As you now know, staying ahead of the change curve and remaining competitive in the job market across the span of your career requires that you go beyond your job description to add increasing value to the organization. What more effective way is there to stand out and perform well than to crack the code of your working life and develop a focused plan to meet the challenges it brings?

The hidden path to success for all of us goes right through the double reality of work. Learning to reveal and transform your hidden curriculum of work resolves the paradox of the double-reality. Doing it over time can make you Future-Proof and give you the best chance at a long, successful working life. Whether your primary focus is working well in your own role, managing people and teams more effectively, or leading an organization toward long-range success, the purpose of this book is to help you expose the true challenges of your work so that you can meet them head-on. The practical tools introduced throughout each chapter are research based and field tested, so whether you are a new grad still waiting for your first day on the job, or are in your third act trying to reinvent your next career, there are valuable insights that you can apply right now to go beyond the job description and get you on the path to success at work.

EXPOSING THE HIDDEN CURRICULUM OF WORK

So what exactly is the hidden curriculum of work? First, a hidden curriculum exists anytime there are two simultaneous challenges where one is visible, clear, and understood and the other is concealed, ambiguous, and undefined. For example, professional athletes master the fundamentals of their sport and excel at the highest level on the court or field of play... but they still have to learn how to deal with wealth, fame, and the many other challenges and distractions that come with professional sports. And, when children enter school, they have to master the educational standards in their curriculum... but, reading, math, and science lessons do not prepare them for the peer pressure, social dynamics, and developmental challenges of youth that they inevitably face. In the same way, *there is a hidden curriculum of work* that we all encounter.

The hidden curriculum of work is different for everybody. No two are the same and so there is no single formula for cracking the code. For example, consider one very common task that often accompanies most job descriptions.

While the precise wording may vary, many of our roles include a function like this: *Work closely with team members and collaborate on projects that achieve department goals and company objectives.* Even if this task is not in your current job description explicitly, it is likely reflected somewhere in your performance expectations. At face value the task sounds pretty simple, but what does it mean to "collaborate" in this department?

To successfully fulfill this role, you must:

- Know your own department's goals and company objectives well enough to recognize what is most important for your team;
- Understand the diverse communication patterns among colleagues, including the various "triggers" to avoid;
- Stay mentally flexible and willing to adapt your own style to ensure open communication and effective responsibility sharing;
- Avoid overcollaborating, but have the wisdom to know what requires healthy discussion and shared decision making; and
- Hold your ground on priorities that matter to the success of the team, and compromise when needed to empower others and maintain productive chemistry with the group.

After reading this task's alternative demands, or the "job-within-the-job," you begin to see the complexities that emerge when you look past the superficial roles and expectations to expose the hidden curriculum of work. While the precise challenges and opportunities vary by situation and context, it is clear that what we read on our job descriptions and business cards, and what we encounter in the actual workplace, are two very different things. This is the *double reality of work* in action.

Returning to the example of the task above—*Work closely with team members and collaborate on projects that achieve department goals and company objectives*—the standard job description likely also lists related skills and experiences that are required to fulfill the responsibilities. For example, it may say: *Must possess effective communication skills and the ability to work well independently and with the larger team.* As commonplace as they are, insubstantial statements like these do little more than restate the task with a few glossy adjectives. And, in the same way that the true demands of the task go unmentioned in the job description, the range of skills and capabilities needed to consistently and effectively meet the hidden curriculum of this task are nowhere to be found. Anyone who has worked within a team has learned the hard way that success requires far more than a generalization like "effective communication" and superficial quips like "be a team player."

Looking at this one simple task and comparing the superficial description with the actual demands brings the hidden curriculum of work into focus. For a fuller picture, we can look at the hidden curriculum of work from the perspective of a full job description. This goes beyond the simple picture portrayed by the lists of tasks and activities in a standard job description and it produces a first look at the more complex "job-within-the-job." To illustrate this here is an actual position description for a typical *Sales Manager* role. As you read each bullet point, notice how the *true challenges of work* are left hidden in plain sight:

- Determines annual unit and gross-profit plans by analyzing trends and implementing related marketing strategies.
- Establishes sales objectives by forecasting and developing annual sales quotas for selected regions.
- Implements national sales programs by developing field sales action plans.
- Maintains sales volume, product mix, and selling price by keeping current with supply and demand, changing trends, economic indicators, and competitors.
- Completes national sales operational requirements by scheduling and assigning employees and following up on work results.
- Builds national sales staff by recruiting, selecting, orienting, and training employees.
- Counsels and disciplines employees, as well as monitors and appraises ongoing performance results.
- Maintains professional and technical knowledge by attending educational workshops, reviewing professional publications, establishing personal networks, and participating in professional societies.
- Contributes to team effort by completing other duties as assigned.

Generic position descriptions such as these litter job boards and websites in many organizations, large and small. While a well-written standard position description does a decent job of describing the tasks, it makes no real reference to the true nature of what is required to get the job done. There is no mention at all of the major elements of the "job-within-the-job" or the skills and abilities required to meet those subtle challenges. What would happen, however, if the same recruitment and selection process was based on a full accounting of the role, including the major elements of the hidden curriculum of work? Table 1.1 shows a side-by-side comparison of what both job descriptions could look like together.

A quick analysis of this side-by-side comparison reveals several important factors. First, when we use a traditional position description as the guide for identifying the right candidates, we fail to look for the full combination of knowledge, skills, and abilities required. If you have ever been in a role that was not a "good fit" then you know how difficult that is. The actual costs of failed recruitments are significant to organizations and teams, and this single factor is among the most reducible costs of doing business. While experience does enable seasoned workers to "read between the lines" and judge for themselves what the true demands of the job really are, it is an unnecessary guessing game that can be avoided.

When you engage in a recruitment and selection process based on the left-hand column you end up getting told the *right answers* from candidates, but you do not get the *real answers*. The job seekers are at the same disadvantage; they weigh their options and the potential fit of the job based upon an ambiguous, beige description of what the job is and what it actually takes to perform well.

YOUR DOUBLE REALITY AT WORK

For a moment, think about the organizations that you have worked for over the years...now walk yourself through the major milestones you achieved there, from the initial recruitment, selection, on-boarding, and orientation, to the training and development, management, and evaluation. *How much did these formal events present you (or your managers) with opportunities to honestly acknowledge, discuss, and gain support for addressing the true challenges of work?*

Now, think about your everyday experiences between these milestones. You undoubtedly spent countless hours assessing your own tasks and priorities

Table 1.1 Side-by-Side Job Descriptions

Traditional Position Description −Sales Manager−	*Job-within-the-Job Description* −Sales Manager−
• Determines annual unit and gross-profit plans by analyzing trends and implementing related marketing strategies.	• Constantly scan industry and market trends to anticipate which marketing strategies will most likely succeed despite many unknown factors…and be willing to make lots of small mistakes and course-correct as conditions change.
• Establishes sales objectives by forecasting and developing annual sales quotas for regions.	• Make an educated guess about your numbers in a way that shows off your contribution, but avoid setting the bar so high that failure gets noticed by headquarters…and effectively manage the politics and pressures of unrealistic expectations held by company leaders who may not have a solid grasp of the region you are responsible for.
• Implements national sales programs by developing field sales action plans.	• Take a systems approach to developing detailed, customized action plans based on national sales strategies and programs…and understand the success drivers in order to leverage your team's talent and to mitigate their weaknesses.
• Maintains sales volume, product mix, and selling price by keeping current with supply and demand, changing trends, economic indicators, and competitors.	• Monitor and integrate hundreds of data points in a way that identifies challenges and opportunities before they derail the balanced implementation of sales strategies.
• Completes national sales and operational requirements by scheduling and assigning employees and following up on work results.	• Handle all of your own work…and stay engaged with your sales team consistently enough to observe their work and direct them as needed so they: address their performance challenges, comply with expected operational procedures, and identify high-risk factors for potential non-compliance.

- Builds national sales staff by recruiting, selecting, orienting, and training employees.

  - Have a clear grasp of the knowledge, skills, abilities, and overall capabilities required to successfully fulfill the role of a sales staff member...navigate an antiquated recruitment and selection process in order to choose the right candidates for the job...and invest whatever time is needed to orient them to the core performance requirements of their job and support their on-the-job training and mentoring.

- Counsels and disciplines employees, as well as monitors and appraises on-going performance results.

  - Go back to basics and make sure each of your team members knows their role, core job requirements, and greatest value contribution to the organization...consistently walk-the-talk about performance by having the honest conversations with all staff...Engage just as frequently with the high achievers as you do with the under achievers.

- Maintains professional and technical knowledge by attending educational workshops, reviewing professional publications, establishing personal networks, and participating in professional societies.

  - Do not ever stop learning if you want to remain relevant. Stay current with the latest best practices in the field and keep yourself on the cutting edge...avoid the "flavor-of-the-month" stuff and find real opportunities for competitive advantage...and do all of this in your spare time because we will not pay you for your professional development.

- Contributes to team effort by completing other duties as assigned.

  - Go beyond your job description and add value to the organization in ways that we can't tell you (because we don't always know what we need).

(trying to figure out which one was most important in the moment), interacting with supervisors and colleagues to negotiate and clarify assignments, and participating in lots of one-on-one and team meetings to communicate through difficulties, coordinate changing goals, and establish priorities for action. Every day that you did these things you also likely tried your best to stay current with the latest job knowledge, maintain good professional relationships, keep an eye out for new opportunities to stand out and make a difference, and enjoy each day at work as much as possible. These dual challenges reflect your hidden curriculum in action.

The fact that everyone in the world of work confronts this double reality, and yet mainstream leadership and organization development best practices fail to account for it, is precisely why I argue for a new way of thinking about work. *It is time to drop the pretense that our standard jobs are the only jobs that matter.*

The fundamental system on which most organizations structure their operations is based on what I call the Standard Model of Work (SMW). Within the SMW there is virtually no acknowledgment of the presence and impact of the hidden side of work. This wholesale failure to recognize the gap between *the way we work* and *the true demands of getting great work done* not only sustains the impact of challenges from the hidden curriculum of work, but it erodes the credibility that leaders maintain as vital resources for problem solving.

While I have encountered leaders who grasp this at a fundamental level, it is still the case that very few organizations actually understand how to equip their leaders and teams with the tools to effectively meet the demands of the hidden curriculum of work. After all, how can they equip their leaders and teams with the tools to effectively meet the true demands of work when there is no open acknowledgment that it exists?

THE HIDDEN CURRICULUM OF WORK UP-CLOSE

Two brief case studies, one individual and one team scenario, are presented here to show you a picture of the hidden curriculum of work up close. By focusing on each of these perspectives you will see the many interconnections between the worker, work team, and workplace levels. And, you will see how a reliance on the SMW can adversely impact the capacity of people to get their best work done.

BILL IS STUCK IN HIS OWN WAY

Bill was a new account representative at a mid-size financial services company. His undergraduate degree in finance had prepared him for the industry, but college classes and two internships had not sufficiently prepared him for the real world of work. According to his job description, Bill was responsible for the presentation and sale of financial products and services to new and existing customers and for ensuring that customers' needs were identified and fulfilled. Specific duties included things like generating activity reports, making sales calls, demonstrating knowledge of regulatory responsibilities, obtaining legal documentation, and gathering required customer information in compliance with related state and federal mandates. The only specific, required skills listed on the position description were three years of college or related work experience; excellent communication skills; and basic computer experience.

The interview went great and the first day on the job was fantastic. The real challenge came on day two, when the manager who had hired Bill left the company abruptly to pursue another opportunity. The "plan" for his orientation and on-the-job-training was scrapped in place of a figure-it-out-yourself approach. The people in his regional office were nice, but they were all busy, and Bill was simply the new guy with bad timing and no manager. The hidden curriculum of work hit him hard and fast.

Bill's days were filled with a mad rush to figure out his own job on the fly. Everything seemed important; as a result, nothing was truly important. All of his priorities blended together, and Bill was never sure if he was doing the right thing. If he needed help understanding how something should be done, he would ask others. The explanations he got referred to *how things have always been done* and if he questioned why, he would hear echoes from the "ghost" of his previous manager, who had set the tone for the company's policies and procedures. So Bill was on his own, responsible for being successful, but stuck in an environment that he could not easily adapt to or change. In addition to these challenges, Bill was committed to developing good working relationships with his new colleagues so he avoided hard questions at meetings to avoid coming across as confrontational. While he surrendered his perspective for the sake of consensus, the answers he needed to do his job well never came.

There was much more to the story, but this provides a glimpse of Bill's hidden curriculum of work as it surfaced. The good news for Bill was that once we worked together to identify his "job-within-the-job," he began to get some positive traction. Each of the struggles that he confronted were quite manage-able once they were seen clearly in the light of day, and his colleagues were more than happy to meet his new requests for a different kind of collabora-tion. The more he faced his true challenges at work, the better he felt about his everyday performance. That virtuous cycle was noticed by his peers and had a multiplier effect on his colleagues in the regional office.

THE MARKETING TEAM IS OUT OF IDEAS

Members of a small but successful creative group were struggling to com-municate during their design meetings. The communication breakdowns became so consistent that the quality of their work suffered and they began losing business as a result of their ineffective pitches to prospective new cli-ents. The firm's work was about advertising and public relations, delivering brand strategy, and building online identity for their clients, but the creative edge was really what they sold. After a particularly frustrating series of new business development meetings, the principal of the firm decided that some-thing had to be done. The pivotal person in all of this was Kevin, the firm's creative director, whose job it was to set the tone for the team's creative ses-sions where great ideas would get transformed into innovative and successful executions.

Over the course of two coaching sessions, I worked with Kevin to explore what was going on and to see whether revealing the team's hidden challenges of work would hold clues to the team's recent decline in performance. In typical fashion, I started with the SMW and got Kevin to tell me about the expecta-tions of his job and the specific roles and functions he delivered. After thinking about his formal job description for a bit, he offered the following list:

> "My job is to lead creative sessions for project kick-offs. I'm always managing multiple projects from concept through completion and I try to build creative programs and design concepts that exceed our client's expectations and advance our own Agency's brand strategy. We want to be known for breaking all of the limits! I establish creative direction for our entire line of services and programs. I supervise our staff and try to manage the broader team of vendors and part-ners and I interface with our account team on administrative details. We are a small firm, so I try to get everyone involved in generating ideas for pitching and proposal writing. At the end of the day though, my job is to provide quality control over concepts and projects."

After hearing this rundown, I asked Kevin to talk about the struggles he faced, and this began to bring to the surface many of his true challenges on the job. Once the light bulbs started going off, I asked him to describe these hidden challenges in his own words, and he said:

"We overcollaborate. There is too much teamwork and that is one of the reasons we are losing our edge. I hired people for a reason and, although it is sometimes good to get others involved in pitch meetings and proposal writings, too many fingers in the pot have created a bottleneck. And, we have had so much success the last two years; we keep sticking with what worked. This effort to repeat our success has left us following a formula, but our clients don't want something we produced last year for some other company. I need to exercise my judgment and course correct earlier so that we do not waste time in bad iteration cycles. We also have overcomplicated things. We are offering several different platforms now and we sometimes talk in such lofty terms—it always comes back to a concept, a message, and a creative way to tell the story. We have to get out of our own way."

This is only a summary of Kevin's experience, but it gives another window into the hidden curriculum of work. When everything you do actually pushes against what you need and want, the results can be frustrating beyond words. The good news for Kevin, like Bill in the first scenario, was that once we worked together to identify the true value he could add, things got better quickly. The increased value that these changes added to the agency was huge, and the impact on his own quality of working life was even greater.

TYPICAL RESPONSES TO THE HIDDEN CURRICULUM OF WORK

By examining the hidden curriculum of work up close you can see the ways in which its subtle challenges quietly lead us into habits of behavior and patterns of communication that prevent our best work. When people begin to recognize that their job isn't what they thought it would be and that the hidden side of work has the potential to undermine their performance, there are often three typical reactions that I see among individuals and teams. None of these response patterns are ideal because in some way they absorb valuable resources and energy and end up sustaining the negative impact of the hidden challenges of work. These three responses include the Head in the Sand approach, Brute Force Problem Solving, and the Calvary Call.

HEAD IN THE SAND

The Head in the Sand approach is an understandable, but highly ineffective, response that requires finding the largest rock available and crawling under it. Along the fight, flight, or freeze continuum of reactions to danger, this is the instinctive reaction associated with flight and freezing. When people are disproportionately outmatched by their hidden curriculum of work and there are no productive resources to balance the equation, this avoidance response is often seen as the only recourse to address challenges that remain well beyond their control. For far too many people who define "surviving" at work as the new "thriving," this is the response that feels like it is the only viable option.

BRUTE FORCE PROBLEM SOLVING

Brute Force Problem Solving is admirable, but exhausting. This approach includes a combination of motivation to make things better *and* frustration at barriers that are constantly felt, but seldom seen. The tactic here is to muscle your way through the barriers of work and to try to outlast them with toughness. While some positive progress can be made, the majority of energy is usually spent resolving the presenting-level issues, so no systemic change occurs. And, there is often collateral damage, as the people involved get bruised by this kind of approach. The reason is that it is really hard to separate the problem from the people involved in it. As a result, Brute Force Problem-Solving can take a toll on relationships when frustrations build and solutions remain elusive.

THE CALVARY CALL

The Calvary Call involves the use of a third party or outside resource to assist with one or more effects of the hidden side of work. Whether it is a coach to address behavioral issues or a consultant to address people/resource/strategy connections, the Calvary effect occurs when you hear the loud swooping sound of a technical or process expert entering the organization for a short time to "fix the situation" and then exiting just as quickly. The focus of their initiatives is often as superficial as the problem identification in the first place. Instead of understanding the root cause of what is going on, there are offers of team building, leadership development, change management tutorials, and lessons on improving communication, managing time and priorities, and dealing with difficult people. While all of these may help in some way, they do not change the systemic challenges sustained by the double reality of work.

Each of these three typical reactions leaves us with *persistent deficit disorder*, which is my way of saying that the stress and challenge of work always seem to be one step ahead of us. Because these typical response patterns deepen the impact of the barriers and sustain our avoidance of the hidden side of work, in turn we are left with no extra margin for meeting the ongoing challenges we face in our working lives. This is why so many people I work with start out feeling overwhelmed, outmatched, and ready to declare the concept of a healthy working life no more than a myth. Each of these three reactions allows the problems of our work to linger, and that leaves us with ongoing baggage that is in a perpetual state of irresolution.

When people experience more demands than they have available resources to meet them, they experience an insufficient margin of power.[3] This low margin eliminates their potential to invest energy and resources in the process of learning and subsequently apply that learning to meaningful action. I call these our *persistent deficits* because they not only preoccupy us (consciously and unconsciously) but they also create a bottleneck that prevents new information and ideas from getting in to help.

A BETTER RESPONSE PATTERN

We need better response patterns to the true demands of work—our individual, team, and organizational success depend on it. Because the complexity and pace of change in the modern world of work show no signs of letting up, the three typical response patterns to work only threaten to make us fall farther behind. The R-I-T-E Model and its associated tools that will be presented throughout the book are built entirely on uncovering the governing dynamics of the problem, so they *solve for pattern.*[4]

This term, coined by the brilliant writer and social critic Wendell Berry, means that insights and solutions can address multiple problems simultaneously, while reducing the creation of new collateral issues. This translates to getting problems solved right the first time and leaving the baggage behind. Cleaning out this bottleneck resolves the inverse equation of *less available time and energy for the things that require more focused effort,* which so often leaves people feeling buried and overwhelmed. Once your persistent deficits are eased, you will clear margin, boost your capacity to deal with new concerns in real-time, and quit stockpiling unresolved barriers and their cumulative, adverse impacts.

THE COST OF THE HIDDEN CURRICULUM OF WORK

You begin your familiar commute to work and as you get closer, that awful feeling stirs in your stomach. "Maybe I'm just tired," you say to yourself. Or, maybe it's that never-ending project that is already scrambling your mind...or it could be that crazy workload that has been stressing you out so much over the past few months...or perhaps you are just a bit nervous about a possible confrontation with someone you have not been getting along with at work. Whatever it is, you find a way to rationalize yourself into the parking lot, out of the car, and through the doors. You make it through the day using a variety of tactics. You keep busy, you avoid challenging situations the best you can, and you try to pick your moments when to care about certain things and when to let others go. Before you know it, you are back in the car, bus, or train, commuting home again from another long day at work. When a trusted friend or family member asks "How was your day?" you say half-jokingly, "*Well, I survived.*"

For far too many people, this story reflects some element of truth regarding the brutal facts of work. I can recount hundreds of coaching conversations with people who were either gearing up for these kinds of challenging days, or decompressing from a string of them after a tumultuous time on the job. In most of these situations where survival becomes the bar for success, the people are not lazy nor are they looking to avoid hard work; they are genuinely in a state of low-grade stress because the *true challenges of work* have eroded the quality of their working lives and sapped their motivation to thrive.

Because the hidden curriculum of work keeps these challenges out of plain sight, the anxiety and stress they cause is ever present, but never fully addressed. The overall productivity costs of this general malaise that so many people experience are incalculable. However, even a modest effort to examine the costs of the "survival mode of work" shows a stark picture of the deficit that it creates, most widely recognized as *disengagement* in work:

- "Seventy-one percent of American workers are 'not engaged' or 'actively disengaged' in their work, meaning they are emotionally disconnected from their workplaces and are less likely to be productive;"[5]
- The Gallup organization estimates that total employee disengagement costs the US economy as much as $350 billion annually;[6]
- Disengaged workers perform less effectively overall and are more likely to fail to meet difficult priorities and miss important deadlines;

- Disengaged workers are more likely to blame other people for problems and take a cynical approach to meeting the challenges of change;
- Disengaged workers are more likely to cause or be associated with service failures and customer complaints;
- Disengaged workers are less likely to innovate or seek creative solutions;
- Disengaged workers are less likely to be champions of their organizations, failing to advocate positively for their company;
- Disengaged workers are more likely to be involved in unresolved conflict at work that undermines the performance and well-being of themselves and their colleagues;
- Disengaged workers are more likely to be absent, ill, and tardy;
- Disengaged workers are more likely to suffer the effects of chronic stress at work; and
- Disengaged workers are more likely to stay in their jobs, even after mentally "quitting."

If you are concerned at all about the level of learning and performance in your organization, this is an important list to pay attention to. Estimates about the percentage of actively disengaged workers vary, but it is likely as high as 15 to 26 percent.[7] And, this is not just an American phenomenon either. Recent studies and surveys show that workers in Britain[8] and France are also increasingly disengaged. So the multibillion dollar question becomes: *What causes this massive disengagement and the collateral damage that results?*

I believe that much of this downward trend can be explained in part by the existence of the hidden curriculum of work. It not only threatens the quality of our working lives, but it makes it difficult to get our best work done and leaves many of us in a perpetual state of underperformance. Because the true challenges of work are not openly understood or discussed, people are left to make sense of it and take action on their own. The three typical response patterns are decidedly ineffective, and we have already seen how they simply allow the adverse impacts from the hidden curriculum of work to fester.

THE TRUE CHALLENGE OF WORK: ADDING VALUE AND BREAKING BARRIERS

I have described the true challenge of work as *the urgent mandate to meet the demands of the hidden curriculum of work*. The two parts of this mandate include: (1) The need to add increasing value to your organization through continuous learning and performance; and (2) The need to identify and resolve the everyday barriers that hinder effective performance on the job. To clarify what both of these elements represent, here is a more detailed description, beginning with the need to add increasing value.

ADDING VALUE

If you were a manager and needed to offer a promotion to one of two candidates, which one would you choose? Candidate #1 is friendly, professional, easy to get along with, coachable, and consistent in her performance. She knows the job well, she shows up, and she gets it done. Candidate #2 is also is friendly, professional, easy to get along with, coachable, and consistent in her performance. She also knows her job well, shows up, and gets it done. But, in addition to this, Candidate #2 anticipates the changing needs of the team, identifies important challenges and opportunities, and takes initiative to address those emerging possibilities with consistent results. Again, you have the choice of promoting only one person, so who gets the job? Both of these candidates are nearly identical, except for the fact that one of them goes beyond their standard job description and the expectations that go with it. My guess is that you would choose Candidate #2 for the job. This single quality (which actually includes a specific mind-set and related capabilities) is the pivotal difference maker when all other factors are equal.

If you were to identify a person who embodied this capacity and then dissected their performance on the job to see the precise combination of attitudes, choices, and behaviors it includes, then you might see the following practices:

1. They not only perform the duties outlined in their standard job description well, but they define their "job-within-the-job" and fulfill those demands too. The impact of this, including the perception to others, is that of a double contribution, which sets the tone for their elevated performance;

2. They are able to listen to others, determine what is necessary and important while observing the changing conditions around them (spotting the challenges and opportunities that emerge), and invent ways to make value-added contributions based on what is most important;

3. They distinguish between "shiny objects" that look interesting, but have no real value, and true opportunities to contribute something

innovative and meaningful that matches their individual, team, and organizational objectives;

4. They integrate diverse, often contradictory points of information in order to assess multiple possibilities and improve the quality of their problem solving and decision making;

5. They see challenges and obstacles they face each day as teaching moments that hold clues to potential improvements;

6. They use this cycle of continuous learning and performance to stay ahead of the change curve;

7. They follow through on commitments and consistently produce high-quality work, which builds trust and respect from others; and

8. They out-effort everyone else and the day is done when the job is done, regardless of what the clock says.

These eight factors reflect a few of the common practices of those who add value beyond their job descriptions and get on the path toward *breakthrough performance*. The other side of the hidden curriculum of work includes identifying barriers to learning and performance that show up in our "job-within-the-job." Part 3 covers this topic extensively, but this basic primer will set the stage.

BREAKING BARRIERS

The workplace is full of challenges. When challenges go unresolved, we stop getting good work done, we lose sight of the things that inspire us, and sometimes we disengage. Too many challenges for too long can cause chronic stress and erode our health and well-being. To address this we have to be able to spot and move beyond barriers and the typical causes of workplace challenges that reduce our ability to engage, creatively solve problems, and continuously learn and perform on the job. Meeting the demands of the hidden curriculum of work requires the resolution of the obvious and unseen issues that threaten individual, team, and organizational success.

Sometimes these issues are referred to as *gaps* or *obstacles*, or they are alluded to in more creative ways, such as "The Things in the Bushes."[9] In general terms, words and phrases such as *learning issues, problems, hiccups, breakdowns,* and *blind spots* all capture the general intent of difficulties. Whatever form they come in, collectively I call these *barriers to workplace learning and performance* and they show up incessantly in cubicles, board rooms, break rooms, and out in the field, ready to erode skills, reduce motivation, and distract from priorities and goals. Some barriers subtly impact everyday communication and decision making, while others are more systemic and have adverse impacts on things such as response patterns to change.

These barriers, which nobody is immune to, cover the spectrum of the *hidden side of work*. They can make it difficult for everything from the smallest, seemingly inconsequential to the largest and most essential aspects of work to get done. Regardless of the industry you work in or the level of experience you may have attained, no individual is immune from the effects of barriers. Nobody can opt out, and blue-, green-, and white-collar workers alike are all required to meet their demanding challenges.

It only takes a minute of reflection to bring focus to your barriers. Think about a typical day at work and some of the everyday challenges you face, and ask yourself the following questions:

- What are the most common obstacles that put you in a state of frustration, stress, or crisis and get in your way of great performance?
- Do your recurring obstacles involve the challenges of coordinating priorities and goals with other team members?
- Are the challenges personal and do they involve your own motivation and capacity to know how to identify and make progress on what is most important?
- Are the obstacles organizational and do they include things about the structure and patterns of communication that shape the organization culture?

These questions represent the start of uncovering challenges within your hidden curriculum of work. Chapter 5 will provide you with a detailed guide for identifying the specific, core barriers that reduce your learning and performance and get in the way of your best work. In the meantime, recognizing the presence of these everyday barriers is the first move in debunking the myth of your working life.

KEY TAKEAWAYS

There is a hidden curriculum of work that we all face. Whether we realize it or not, we are working two jobs: the position we were hired to fill plus our "job-within-the-job" that is riddled with challenges to our success. Failing to recognize the stressful impact of the hidden curriculum of work reduces engagement and impacts individual, team, and organizational performance. The hidden path to success for everyone goes right through this double reality of work, which is the gap between what we expect to see and what we actually experience. Learning to expose and transform your challenges of work can make you Future-Proof and give you the best chance at a long, successful working life. The remaining chapters in part 1 provide the rest of the foundation you need for understanding the true demands of your work and preparing you to see your hidden curriculum of work for the first time.

Chapter 2

RETHINKING THE WAY WE WORK

WHILE MOST ORGANIZATIONS CAREFULLY SELECT, train, and support their people to meet the challenges of the jobs they are hired to fill, I have yet to encounter an organization that hires, trains, and manages people based on the realities of the *hidden curriculum of work*. In fact, the fundamental system on which organizations structure their operations is based on what I call the Standard Model of Work (SMW), and there is virtually no formal acknowledgment of the presence and impact of the hidden side of work. This fundamental oversight can drive people crazy.

There is a reason work can be so frustrating and this is it: we are all working two jobs, and as we politely get down to the business of fulfilling the tasks and activities in our primary job descriptions, we incessantly bump up against the real challenges of our "job-within-the-job." And yet, there is no common language to describe this hidden side of work, so we do not speak about it. And because we do not speak about it, we are not given support to address it. And this is the ferocious cycle that ensues from A to D and back again: (A) we are hired and paid to do a job, (B) but are only given a partial picture of what is needed to succeed at it, (C) so we are on our own to understand the missing part of the picture and to figure out our own path toward success, and (D) while all of this unfolds we will not be rewarded any differently if we succeed, but we could still face consequences if we fail to meet the job's demands.

While experience on the job sharpens our capacity to see and respond to some of the hidden challenges of work, discovering these through slow-winding experience and trial-and-error learning can take away from productivity and leave us vulnerable to significant performance failures.

Within the SMW there is a serious traffic jam in the pursuit of improvements to the way we get work done. Perhaps your existing tool chest of resources is already overflowing with unused and ineffective "solutions to the problems of work." A study by the American Society for Training and Development revealed that $125.9 billion are spent each year on employee learning and development initiatives.[1] But because these programs are stuck within the inherent limits of the SMW, by and large they fail to address the true challenges of the hidden curriculum of work.

We need to rethink the way we work. This starts with a realistic assessment of the true challenges of work and a real commitment to exposing the hidden side of work for individuals, leaders, and their teams. This commitment means rethinking the way we write job descriptions, interview and select candidates, orient and train new hires, create performance measures and accountabilities, and develop systems to manage, retain, and promote top performers. (Part 5 of this book reflects this global perspective and provides recommendations on leadership and organization development systems changes that relate directly to these kinds of structural processes and systems.)

When I consult with organizations and their leaders I often introduce the need for this paradigm shift by explaining the vicious cycle described above. Forgetting about the toll that this kind of environment takes on people for the moment, I ask them questions like:

- What do you think the quality of work is likely to be when people are blind to their greatest challenges?
- How much time and energy do you think people spend figuring out their own work when the tasks and activities in their job descriptions are not always relevant or complete?
- What is the total cost to your organization when your entire system of hiring, managing, and evaluating people does not reflect the full spectrum of capabilities and roles you actually need for your business to succeed?

Conversations that flow from questions such as these create an opening for me to compare the difference between the *SMW* and a *new approach to work* that reflects the challenges from the hidden side of work. In order to clarify that distinction in more detail, here are some additional ways of thinking about the SMW.

THE SMW

The way most organizations manage the work of getting their work done follows the SMW. This status quo does a great job of reflecting the presenting conditions of work, such as workflow and administrative needs, communication and reporting functions, and the basic coordination of tasks and activities. However it is an abject failure at recognizing the impacts and demands of the hidden curriculum of work.

When contrasted with an accurate picture of the true challenges of work, the SMW neither reflects an honest picture of work, nor does it play a meaningful role in facilitating improved individual or team performance. On the contrary, the case study that comes next will demonstrate the vast difference between the SMW and a new approach that accurately reflects the hidden curriculum of work.

Imagine how you would feel if you spent most of your day dealing with the effects of a problem at work that went unacknowledged by everyone around you. Because of this, you couldn't talk about it, and there would be no formal resources made available to address it. Although solving this problem would make your life easier, your manager and coworkers don't even consider it. This scenario is an everyday reality for many people on the job because of the fact that the SMW is largely built upon the assumption that our standard jobs are what matter, while our "job-within-the-job"—and all of its hidden challenges—pokes at our progress, nags at our motivation, and gets in the way of our best work.

Ironically, it is the hidden side of work and its many barriers to learning and performance that so often dominate our time and demand most of our energy, attention, and resources. In order to demonstrate this, consider the timeline of Charles's major milestones in his world of work.

A NEW APPROACH TO THE WAY WE WORK

This case tells the story of Charles and Marley. Charles was the newest addition to a team of dynamic professionals working in the hospitality industry. He was eager, focused, and hopeful about his new role that got him in the door with a successful company. His manager, Marley, also cared about Charles's success and was quite committed to her entire team. Despite these good intentions all around, Charles's failure to perform effectively threatened his ongoing employment with the company and caused a crisis of confidence for Marley, who was bewildered by her inability to "manage the newest team member."

I provided executive coaching for both Marley and Charles, and this case study begins with a description of what happened before I began to work with the two of them. You will see that their approach in each of the four stages followed the SMW, which quickly got things off track. The second half of the case study shows how they conducted the "do over" with an acknowledgment of the hidden curriculum of work in each of the four stages.

STAGE #1: THE JOB INTERVIEW

During the job interview process, Marley, the hiring manager, and her selection committee tried to figure out whether Charles was going to be a good fit for the position and a match for the organization. They presented him with a position description; however it only outlined the tasks, responsibilities, and general qualifications required. It did not reveal the true challenges of the role, nor did it elaborate on the required skills to meet those demands. As a skilled interviewer, Marley asked some telling questions that moved things past a superficial screening. However, the SMW reflected both in the job description and interview questions limited the extent to which the nuanced challenges of the job were openly discussed. This translated into a semi-blind-date for both Charles and Marley.

In his last job Charles worked in a similar position, so he was able to use that past experience to answer questions intelligently about the nature of the work and what he would do to succeed at the job. Because these questions were mainly about tasks and activities, the depth of the dialogue only got as far as prescriptions for things like "*managing time effectively* with to-do lists" and "successfully resolving a conflict with a colleague by *speaking your mind honestly.*" This was all that Marley needed to make an educated guess about Charles's ability to succeed, so she hired him on the spot. At no time was there any confirmation that Charles understood the true nature of the job, or that he would be able to identify the challenges to getting results and navigate the various pitfalls that he would likely encounter along the way.

STAGE #2: THE FIRST 90 DAYS

Charles shadowed a colleague for three days, which was the sum total of his orientation and on-the-job training. He had about two hours worth of meetings with Marley over his first two weeks, during which she answered key questions, but admittedly there was precious little capacity building to help him acclimate. He did have the official company orientation to polices, including all of the "P's" (i.e. paychecks, passwords, parking, people, and problems to avoid). And, while these mandatory sessions provided important indicators of the social cues to watch in the workplace, they did little to actually help Charles do his best work.

Charles learned the P's and followed their protocols, Marley made assumptions about his progress and was too busy to notice how he was doing, so he passed through his introductory period (the first 90 days on the job). Although the human resources department in the company advised all direct managers to provide feedback at the conclusion of a new employee's trial period, Marley did not check in with him. Even if she had, it may not have been helpful because the design of the feedback tool was based on the SMW and essentially reflected back the tasks and activities in the job description with generic scales (i.e., Exceeds Expectations, Meets Expectations, Below Expectations, etc.) to rank performance. Although a few difficult challenges from the "job-within-the-job" began showing up, there was nothing Charles did in his first 90 days to get much negative attention.

STAGE #3: IN THE SWING OF THINGS

After about six months it was safe to say that Charles was not new anymore. He was a bright guy so he quickly learned what was taboo and undiscussable at work (based on the cultural norms of the organization and the particular preferences of his manager) and what fair play was. All of this just helped him to blend in.

Because he was not hired, trained, or managed in a way that exposed the hidden curriculum of work, he had to learn things the hard way about what was really required in his role and what credible success would entail. While several helpful colleagues shared their hard-earned wisdom here and there, he was basically on his own to navigate his everyday challenges with as little collateral damage as possible. However, the collateral damage began piling up as he faced two unforeseen challenges in his "job-within-the-job."

First, there were a variety of influential people that needed to have buy-in before any change was implemented. Without knowing who these people were and how to best interact with him, efforts to implement new practices always stalled out due to resistance. Second, the culture of the company was more like the traditional hospitality industry insofar as his working periods were long, included late hours, weekends, and some holidays. Although he had worked in a similar industry and in a related position, his experience was more of a "9 to 5" type, and the stamina and balance he needed in the new job was off kilter.

As a result of these and other related issues, he was not performing very well. But because Charles was successful in fulfilling the basic duties that came naturally to him, he still managed to fly under the radar with no direct conversation with Marley about his successes, challenges, or areas requiring ongoing support. Despite the apparent lack of trouble on the outside, things were not going well. As Charles later put it, "I was suffering in silence using any manner of avoidance tactics and work-around strategies to make sure that those challenges didn't sink me. The whole thing was just exhausting. I knew something had to give."

STAGE #4: CLIMBING OR STAGNATING

For some people, the one-year anniversary of a job results in the beginning of their climb to bigger and better opportunities within the organization. This was not the case for Charles; he was stagnating. Marley was increasingly frustrated with the lack of results that she described as "basic parts of the job" but which Charles was not aware of as priorities. Marley had hired Charles because of his previous experience in a similar role, so she assumed that his lack of productivity was a result of laziness or failure to focus. In reality, the double challenge of Charles's "job-within-the-job" was finally catching up.

He had learned to do the obvious and easy things well, which helped him meet basic expectations and fly under the radar. However, he had failed to learn about the unexpected challenges of working with difficult customers and partnering internally with colleagues to leverage resources and opportunities for growth. As a result he got bogged down and was stagnating in his performance. The quality of his working life also steadily declined. Marley was keen to deliver the truth to him during his annual review, including the fact that he would not be considered for growth opportunities and could be terminated.

This is around the time when I met Marley and began working with her. Getting the working relationship with Charles back on track was one of her biggest priorities so we started by looking at the annual review she was about to give him. After I read it, I noticed that instead of painting a clear picture of his current performance and what he would need to do in order to succeed now and into the future, it simply followed the SMW and did little more than reinforce the same set of superficial requirements that marked his entry into the organization. In the section of the review that was intended to define concrete goals for improvement, Marley only had her vague sense of the core issues to inform her feedback. (She had written: "Charles needs to improve in his overall productivity. He must develop a better structure to his work day in order to meet key priorities and maintain effective relationships with partners.") While the frustration was clear in her feedback, a clarified picture of the precise performance gap was not. Marley's solution was going to be just another addition to her problem. The hidden curriculum of work was threatening to sink Charles, and she had not been effective in her role of helping him to see that.

Now take a look at how they handled their "do over" after being coached to intentionally bring the hidden curriculum of work into their everyday discussions. Astute readers may have noticed how many of Charles's issues were at least in part due to a failure of his manager to actively engage and prepare him for success. After developing a new mind-set and skill set for how she would manage her direct reports, this is the "script" that Marley and I created. She used this with Charles as a refresh to their working relationship, and it is the process she continues to use effectively with every new hire.

STAGE #1: THE JOB INTERVIEW

"Thank you for your interest in our organization, Charles. The goal of this interview is to introduce you to the everyday tasks and activities that will become your responsibility if you are offered and choose to accept this position. Because these tasks and activities only explain part of the picture, we are going to take time to elaborate on what we feel are the true challenges of succeeding in this role. We will not only be very honest with you about what these challenges are, but we will also carefully describe the knowledge, skills, and abilities that a successful candidate needs to meet those demands.

To assist us, we have included current and past team members who have been in the same position and who have learned about the many unexpected challenges that can arise. We know that in the long run you will feel most successful if you are doing your best work, so we want to make sure you have every opportunity to evaluate this opportunity accurately. While this may be quite different from other job interviews, we feel that this approach will give both you and us the chance to judge if this is the right fit."

STAGE #2: THE FIRST 90 DAYS

"Welcome to the team! Simply put, my job as your manager is to help you succeed at work. I know that you will be engaged in what you are doing and that our team and organization will benefit from your quality performance if I am effective. To start, please use the next three months to learn as much as you can about what is required to succeed in this role and deliver your best work. As you figure out what is missing in the standard position description, I would like you to create a secondary job description that maps out the specific challenges behind each major task/activity. I also want you to identify the things you do (or don't do) that reflect the attitudes, behaviors, and choices that help you meet these challenges. As you identify these challenges and the necessary capabilities to meet them, I will work closely with you to acquire additional education, training, and capacity-building resources to equip you for success. I will be honest and open with you throughout this process, and that is the kind of communication and collaboration I expect of you as well...

Congratulations, you competed your introductory period! Our goal during this formal performance review is to exchange perspectives about what has happened over the last quarter. I am very interested in your own evaluation of what you have done well and where you see the need for continued improvement. My responsibility as your manager is to listen to your perspective, as well as to deliver specific performance improvement feedback that acknowledges what is going well and challenges you to improve in specific areas for growth. Rather than using a traditional performance evaluation model that reduces my feedback into vague categories, we will use an alternative model that reflects the expectations and accountabilities of both your job and your "job-within-the-job." Since we have been engaged in frequent, open communication over the last few months, none of this should be a surprise to you."

STAGES #3–4: IN THE SWING OF THINGS & CLIMBING

Thankfully for both Marley and Charles, things got back on track. Charles got into the swing of things, and after the initial challenges of the first few weeks and months, he was climbing in the organization. Both manager and employee truly changed the way they worked.

Charles got a "second interview" that empowered him to really look inside the standard job description to see the "job-within-the-job" that caused him so many headaches. For example, he invested time strategizing ways to more effectively interact with key people. Rather than seeing his efforts to implement new practices stall out due to their resistance, Charles was able to connect with people, better understand the nature of his critical relationships, and act more persuasively with regard to his priorities. Because he had already been confronted by the brutal facts of his unexpected challenges at work, he had a running start on this process. His manager was now supportive of his ongoing learning and performance and he felt free to make small mistakes if it helped to eventually expose and resolve barriers to his productivity. Rather than going home at the end of the day beating himself up about his struggles, Charles was renewed in his confidence and excited about showing up each day.

Marley was also considerably more engaged with Charles, and their discussions about the true priorities of the job were finally honest and direct. Despite the need for additional time, Marley knew that it was a value addition because she was spending more time proactively addressing priorities rather than worrying about them going unmet. She also recognized that the investment on the front end would mean a much more independent, high-performing team, so her investment of time and energy into actively engaging with staff was sustainable in the long run.

DECEPTIVELY SIMPLE, SURPRISINGLY COMPLEX

The case of Marley and Charles reveals one of the most startling aspects of the hidden curriculum of work: it is deceptively simple and surprisingly complex. For example, if we focus on Marley we can apply a bit of common sense and conclude that she could have easily overcome some of her challenges with greater engagement when Charles was brand new. Likewise, we could argue that Charles would have helped his own cause with more assertive requests for support in his first 90 days. While these changes would have been useful to both of them, the "surprisingly complex" part of all this is that the pace of work, the lack of focus on priorities, and their failure to recognize the steadily eroding performance were all so tightly intertwined that they were not noticed. The hidden curriculum of work is hidden in plain sight.

My work as a consultant often begins in these moments where the glaring set of challenges appears like an overwhelming, impossible situation that is hard to define, let alone resolve. In order to get past the paradox of "Deceptively Simple, Surprisingly Complex," we need to move beyond the presenting side of the unwanted experience.

When I begin a coaching or consulting engagement I often begin with a Discovery Session that allows the players to candidly share their starting assumptions and perspectives about "the problem." Over the last several years I have interviewed a wide variety of both individual contributors and experienced managers and leaders from a variety of industries. To find out what they think about their challenges at work, I frame the first part of my discovery session with the question: *"What do you think is going on here . . . and if you had to name the core issue, what would you say the greatest challenge really is?"*

Prior to any formal introduction to the hidden curriculum of work or my system for helping people go beyond their job descriptions, I carefully consider their reflections on the challenges they face in their everyday working lives because they represent the starting place to counter their assumptions about the SMW. Here are a few of the recurring statements I hear about the most common range of issues:

- "Communication is one of the greatest challenges we face. When it goes right we're okay, but when it goes wrong things go off the rails fast."
- "Honestly, we are bombarded with so many things that all look important, it is hard to know what really matters. I don't think that we know what to focus on."
- "Change is the hardest for us. Our industry has been slammed with new regulations and policy changes at the federal level that have upended things. There was already a constant stream of change before, but now these legislative changes and the impacts of the down economy have everyone feeling like they just can't change anymore."
- "As a manager, the hardest thing for me is finding time. I know that the people who work for me need my attention, but I just can't give them the kind of support they need. I don't need a 360-feedback tool because I already know they would say they feel like they're on their own."
- "I see our greatest challenge as a lack of motivation. It seems like people aren't willing to innovate or contribute effort beyond the bare minimum. While I understand that things have been stressful around here for quite a while, the lack of engagement and inspiration zaps possibilities."
- "The problem here is our leaders. They say one thing, but our policies and culture suggest another. I don't think that people can fully trust that there is a plan and that the average employee fits into that image of the future. With the last few unexpected cutbacks, people are concerned for their livelihoods."

These descriptions are telling, they are absolutely true from the perspectives of the people who live them, and talking through them undoubtedly serves as a useful exercise. However, if you dissect each statement, you notice that they only reflect *the presenting conditions* of what happens when the hidden challenges of work run wild. Each problem statement reflects a common aspect of the day-to-day reality of organizational life, but this is only the tip of the iceberg. I have spent my career learning how to listen to statements like this and then quickly and accurately drill down to the systemic causes and conditions that hold these unwanted experiences and outcomes in place. Time and again this pursuit leads back to core barriers to the "job-within-the-job."

To highlight the shift that occurs when you look past the SMW, see what happens when your perspective goes from describing *the tasks and activities* that make up our working days to describing *the hidden side of work*. The left-side of table 2.1 reflects the SMW and the right-side reflects the true demands of the hidden curriculum of work.

Breakthrough performance is only possible with a blended focus on these two columns. The stuff of work includes both sides of this double reality, and while the right-hand side may have more value, the left-hand side cannot be neglected. Once you realize the SMW has failed you by only revealing part of the picture, then you "get it." When that clicks, you can use this new approach

Table 2.1 Describing the Hidden Side of Work

Tasks and Activities in the SMW	The Hidden Curriculum of Work
"Every day at work I…	"Every day at work I…
1. Answer phone and e-mail messages and correspond with others;	1. Share vital information required for effective decision making;
2. Plan my own work;	2. Scan the environment to assess whether my priorities, goals, and related work plans are still relevant;
3. Attend meetings, coordinate tasks and projects with others;	3. Attend meetings to invest time in building relationships that I need to get my best work done *and* I avoid unnecessary teamwork and collaboration that wastes time;
4. Attend presentations and training programs; and	4. Look for ways to continuously learn and improve my performance, whether formal or informal, *and* I pay attention to my own personal development so that I stay engaged in what I am doing; and
5. Measure and evaluate progress.	5. Deliberately partner with others to update our strategy and planning frequently.

to work to accomplish some of the most vital necessities of today's changing world of work, including:

1. Change your organization's culture from within;
2. Transform troubled relationships;
3. Develop more resilience in the face of adversity;
4. Shift conflict effects from damaging to constructive;
5. Share information to limit assumptions;
6. Get collaborative decision making right;
7. Make sense of complexity and ambiguity;
8. Integrate creativity, diversity, and innovation in everyday interactions;
9. Keep people on the same page during periods of intense change; and
10. Increase levels of workplace trust and employee engagement.

KEY TAKEAWAYS

The fundamental system on which organizations structure their operations is based on the Standard Model of Work (SMW), which fails to acknowledge the presence and impact of the hidden side of work. In most organizations the SMW is an unquestioned part of how things are done. Job descriptions are written, interviews are conducted, training and orientation sessions are completed, performance reviews are given, and the cycle continues without formally acknowledging an honest picture of the true challenges of work.

In the SMW there is no common language to describe the hidden side of work. Because it is undiscussable, a vicious cycle ensues: (A) we are hired and paid to do a job, (B) but are only given a partial picture of what is needed to succeed at it, (C) so we are on our own to understand the missing part of the picture and to figure out our own path toward success, (D) and while all of this unfolds we will not be rewarded any differently if we succeed, but we could still face consequences if we fail to meet its demands.

In order to create a performance advantage for individuals and teams, a realistic assessment of the true challenges of work and a commitment to exposing the hidden side of work is needed. This commitment will overcome the paradox of "Deceptively Simple, Surprisingly Complex" because it enables you to look past the presenting side of work at the true nature of the challenge.

Chapter 3

AVERAGE IS OVER

FOLLOWING THE ECONOMIC AND FINANCIAL crisis of 2008, work became more competitive than ever, and job insecurity had never been higher. Thought leaders like Thomas Friedman and others clearly said that "average is over, and everyone must find their 'extra' in order to stay relevant."[1] Despite the numerous calls for rethinking how we approach the challenges of work, there have been surprisingly few definitive, research-based solutions.

In this post-average economy, those who know how to reveal opportunities for improved learning and performance will meet the challenge of change, stay relevant at work, and give themselves the best chance for long, successful working lives. Organizations that are filled with Future-Proof leaders and teams—those who create systems that increase the capacity of their people to transform the hidden challenges of work into opportunities for improved learning and performance—will win in the market.

The purpose of this chapter is to definitively establish the urgency and commitment you need to stay focused on your path to success at work. It sets a deeper context regarding the changes in work, including the value of your capacity to go beyond your job description and achieve *breakthrough performance*.

YOUR WORKING LIFE

Our modern lives are working lives. People start working sooner and delay retirement longer. For example, I got my first job—at age seven—at the *Gold Rush Gazette* newspaper where I peddled black-and-white broadsheets to tourists in the historic mining town of Columbia, California. I sold each paper for 50 cents, and my deal with the publisher included a generous 50/50 split.

I continued to invent jobs like this one in the informal economy until I reached the official working age of 15, when I began a formal progression of roles that has led me to this moment.

According to present-day estimates regarding our career paths, the average person will have **4–6** different careers reflected by **10–15** specific jobs with more than **8–10** different companies.[2]

Considering the current life expectancy for Gen X'ers like me, as well as the present downward trend in the economy, if I keep my health and wits about me then I will most likely work until I am 75 years old. If we consider the implications of current biotechnology research and medical advances that could improve health beyond current levels, the millennial generation and those that follow are likely to live and work well into their 100s. For me, the anticipated 70 years spent in the workplace make a definitive, statement about the adage *life is work* and *work is life*.

The new reality for each of us is a working life that will extend over six to seven decades. Our work spans will include a constant, mutually reinforcing relationship between our health at work and the overall quality of our lives. Just like the day-to-day micro choices, habits, beliefs, and values we embrace affect our overall quality of life, each of us has a set of decisions to make at work that will directly enhance or erode the quality of our working lives.

Embracing the idea of a working life should trigger some practical and profound questions for you:

- Will I remain employable as society, culture, and technology inevitably change around me?
- How can I continually enhance my skills to stay competitive in the job market?
- Will I adapt my knowledge, skills, and abilities to add increasing value to my organization . . . or will I plateau and get passed by others who are younger, smarter, and hungrier than me?
- How can I craft a working life full of meaningful experiences, instead of just doing my time?

Beyond these individual questions, there are also hard questions facing teams such as:

- How can colleagues understand each other when things get complex and change so often?
- How can we leverage our conflict and challenges, rather than have them set us back?

At the organization-wide level, the critical questions include:

- How can we get off of the change treadmill and proactively create the conditions for our success?
- How can we build a deep bench of talent that is flexible enough to shift with our emerging opportunities?
- How can we motivate individuals to take full responsibility for their own growth and development?

Even if you have been tempted to just "punch the clock" and go through the motions, all you have to do is a little bit of math to see that it is worth a small investment of time and energy to make incremental changes in your working life *now* so that it pays dividends *for years to come*. Learning how to navigate your hidden curriculum of work early can pay dividends longer. Figure 3.1 shows the investment curve, including the powerful trajectory that your entire working life can follow, if you make an investment in getting Future-Proofed right now.

The Greek god Proteus was known to instantly change shape to adapt to the dangers of changing circumstances. The mandate for employees to continuously adapt their skills to meet changing demands offers an unmistakable parallel: today's careers need to be more *Protean*. In response to the range of challenges presented by both the new economy and the evolving workplace, organizations now demand that all workers continually learn and adapt, developing not just the needed technical skills, but also the mental flexibility, self-motivation, and psychological mobility needed to thrive and maintain job security in a fast-changing, globalized world.[3]

WORK IS FAST, CHANGING, AND RELENTLESS

Thirty-five years ago, asking somebody the question "What do you do for work?" was still a pretty straightforward exchange. It was mostly the consultants, financial services professionals, and "weirdoes" out in California's Silicon Valley who could answer the question and still leave you confused. Now, all

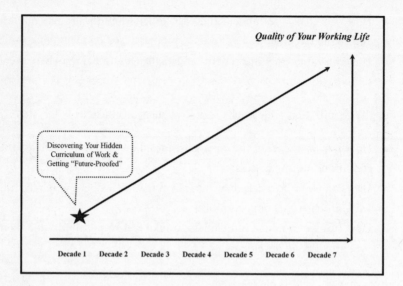

Figure 3.1   The Investment Curve in Your Working Life.

work is fast, changing, and relentless. Many jobs that were once taken for granted are disappearing, while new ones emerge in the increasingly gray areas that were not even on the organization chart a few years ago.

The sudden ambiguity around how we define work is in large part due to the fact that things are more fluid and unpredictable than ever. The roiling white water of today's organizations reflects the constant state of change that workers and teams face. Peter Vaill, the influential organizational change theorist, had a way of describing the simplicity within the complexity of organizational life. In this regard, I appreciate Vaill's[4] vivid metaphor, which describes "white water" as an onslaught of surprises, constant ambiguity, and continuously emerging problems.

"Organizational life takes place in permanent white water."[5]

In 2005, the prolific columnist and commentator on global economic and business trends Thomas Friedman[6] described this scenario in much different terms. His metaphor was a flat world, where everything and everyone is connected. In this world, businesses need workers of all persuasions to be adaptable to changing circumstances, differentiated in their roles, and relational and multidimensional in their problem solving. Because of the intense competitive pressures and the never-ending pursuit of technological breakthroughs, today's workforce has to be leaner and more agile, more focused on identifying value from the customer perspective, and more proactive about developing innovative strategies to exploit this value. Friedman's 2012 update restated the impact of these trends on everyday workers in starker terms: "…everyone needs to find their extra—their unique value contribution that makes them stand out in whatever is their field of employment."[7]

Whether you prefer the metaphor of a flat world or that of raging rapids full of white water, it is clear that above all else, workers must be continuous learners locked faithfully in the pursuit of new knowledge, skills, and abilities that keep them on the *right* side of the edge of relevance.

Integrating these two metaphors illustrates how success in the workplace is also now more dependent on emotional intelligence and other soft skills. The psychologist Robert Kegan[8] explored the impact of advances in the mental complexity of life, suggesting that workers today are expected to invent their own roles; be self-initiating, self-correcting, and self-evaluating; be guided by their own visions of work; and take responsibility for what happens both internally and externally within the organization. This expanding directive paints a picture of work today that differs from expectations and roles from even a generation ago. Considering these trends, the effective acquisition, creation, and application of new forms of knowledge is critical for employees to remain vital in the contemporary workplace.[9]

Learning how to identify and navigate the hidden curriculum of work is *the* competitive advantage of the twenty-first century. It is a systemic approach to work that responds to the changing demands of individuals and leaders to create their own roles and accumulate the essential skills and abilities to succeed in an environment of uncertainty.

Although any number of additional competitive advantages can serve as critical business success factors, it is the strength of an organization's workforce—its human capital—that serves as a foundation for its capacity to achieve its intended purpose. Human capital specifically refers to the sum total of knowledge, experience, and performance capability that an organization can access to create wealth. In essence, the more effectively an organization manages its human capital resources, the more successful it is likely to be.[10]

Today, most people are knowledge workers tasked with doing service-driven work. What we made used to matter; however, what we know, how we work, and the value of the services we offer matter most now. Perhaps in the best position to comment on the changing nature of work is the father of modern management, Peter Drucker,[11] who predicted and then watched as the future of work changed over five decades of writing and researching in favor of the knowledge worker.

Knowledge itself is not of any intrinsic value, however. Only through the consistent and targeted application of knowledge can we derive real value. In today's service-driven and knowledge-empowered workplace, everyone has to embrace the soft skills associated with developing and sustaining effective interpersonal relationships. This requirement extends to the traditionally technical fields like manufacturing, engineering, and computer science, as well as to the traditionally "people-friendly" roles filled by project managers, sales and customer service experts, and collaborative team leaders, among others.

These changes in the nature of work are not momentary trends or generational anomalies either. For the first time in our history we have five different generations working together simultaneously. There has been much ado about this, including many cautionary tales about the differences between them and the things leaders can do to accommodate the stereotypical needs of the oldest (i.e., entrenched, afraid to change) and youngest (i.e., entitled, too quick to change) among us. The hidden curriculum of work transcends these generational trends. Decoding the hidden side of work is not something that only the new generation needs to accomplish in order to succeed at work, nor are the related skills required to navigate the hidden curriculum of work solely reserved for the seasoned veterans of the workforce to stay relevant and avoid being left behind. While learning to navigate the hidden curriculum of work provides a significant competitive advantage to both of these cohorts (as well as to the ones in between), it is an unavoidable aspect of working life that everyone, regardless of age or tenure in the world of work, must face.

All of these changes combined have led to a very clear distinction about *the greatest technology.* It is not the latest device or software application; it is human capital. Although any number of additional competitive advantages can serve as critical business success factors, what consistently serves as the foundation of an organization's capacity to achieve its intended purpose is the strength of its workforce and the ability to tap the full measure of potential within its collective human capital. The organizations that win will be the ones full of Future-Proof workers who can withstand the white water and thrive in a flat world where average is over.

WHY YOU NEED TO GO BEYOND YOUR JOB DESCRIPTION

Now, unlike any time in the past, your own ongoing employability comes from your capacity to independently and consistently add increasing value to the organization, not simply from your title or tenure in the organization. as it may have been in the past. However, the economic and market changes that put increasing pressures on organizations to cut costs and take short-term avenues to improve the balance sheet have shifted the onus of responsibility for learning *from the employer* directly to the *employee*. As employees are held increasingly accountable for obtaining their own job-related knowledge, they must initiate and follow through on their own growth and development opportunities.

Translation: you are your own human resources department. And for that matter, you may be your own trainer, coach, and career development strategist.

While some companies still understand and operate with the knowledge that investing in their employees' development can be a significant source of competitive advantage, in many cases workers today are more or less on their own. The influential speech-writer turned thought leader Dan Pink[12] calls us "free agents," and the management consulting guru Tom Peters[13] writes about this phenomenon as "the brand called you." Whatever we call it, the fact is we are now responsible for finding new and different ways to add value by increasing our knowledge, skills, and abilities.

In the past things moved slowly enough that it was feasible to be completely outmatched by your "job-within-the-job" and still survive in the organization. Now, however, it is no longer an option to just focus on your first job and simply wish that the challenges of your second job would fade away. The competitive pressures of a global economy and rising job insecurity combine to form a stark reality—add value, or risk being left behind.

When we put a spin of adventure on this new reality, it can sound pretty good:

> *You are alone on the frontier, blazing a career pathway with your own passion and talent. Life-long careers are dead, and you have embraced the "free agent mentality" with full vigor…*

Ideally, this vision is inspiring. However, in reality, it can be difficult to sustain on pure idealism. You know you need to stay ahead of the change curve, but you already have a full plate. Should you hire a coach? Should you get an additional certification? Should you go back to school for that MBA or other advanced degree? What can you do to stand out in the crowd without changing your entire life circumstances to do it?

My answer to these questions for most people is *no,* across the board. Instead, I say Future-Proof yourself. To illustrate this, let's take a look at two people (both named Fred) to understand what getting Future-Proofed is really about.

A Lesson from Fred

Old Fred...

Arrived at the office at 9:00 am on a Monday and the same roles and responsibilities would await him. Following his coffee and donut, he would delve into the same routines and tasks that formed his experience. If Fred played by the rules he would continue showing up each day for 30 years, possibly achieve a few promotions, and then retire after a semi-distinguished career in the same industry, with the same company.

Sorry Fred, things have changed in the workplace and they will never be the same. What you experienced as job security, predictability in your role, and the slow and steady march of technology are gone. Now, you and billions of other male and female workers face a dramatically different experience.

...Future-Proof Fred

New Fred almost never leaves the office. His smart phone is always on and through a complex platform of software he can be anywhere, anytime and do most anything virtually. The office might be a coffee shop or a spare room in the house. Regardless of where Fred does his work, information will already have found its way to a laptop, cell phone, or tablet. Real-time information is readily available and is a key factor in determining where he'll place time, energy, and resources that day.

If Fred does report to the office, each day looks different. New Fred will make a series of critical judgments about what is most important as he sets the trajectory for the day's goals. A typical day could include meetings, one-to-one discussions, large group presentations, and individual time transitioning from one activity to the next. Fred will scramble to be productive by rolling with change and inventing ways to add increasing value to his team and to the organization as a whole.

This is why Fred—and everybody else—must get future-proofed. For new Fred, each day is a barrage of often-contradictory pieces of information that will require high levels of cognitive processing, multitasking, and emotionally demanding routines such as prioritizing known and unknown factors, real-time decision making, and continuous opportunity analysis to make the best choices regarding who to collaborate with and what action to take. The most striking difference between old/new Fred is that new Fred will likely hold about 15 different jobs – each one requiring him to reinvent his role and contribution again and again.

If we take a closer look at the true challenge of your work, including Fred's reaction to it, we see some of the specific skills required to meet these challenges and get Future-Proofed. These skills will be addressed in chapters 11 and 14 more fully. However, an initial take includes the ability to:

- Remain flexible with change and understand when to pivot, and when to hold steady;
- Think critically to challenge potentially faulty assumptions;
- Persuade people to create support for ideas;
- Build rapport and strong relationships for collaborating effectively;
- Leverage disagreement for diversity and innovation;
- Make sense of different viewpoints to enhance meaning; and
- Motivate self and others.

Fred's experience navigating the changing nature of work, confronting the hidden challenges of his "job-within-the-job," and basic efforts to maintain some kind of balance between work and life is no easy task.

NAVIGATING THE TRUE DEMANDS OF THE JOB: *THE* COMPETITIVE ADVANTAGE OF THE TWENTY-FIRST CENTURY

The term *competitive advantage* refers to any factor(s) that can be leveraged to stand out, get ahead, and *win* in a given pursuit. In business, competitive advantage matters significantly when you operate in a climate of hypercompetition with ever-increasing costs of doing business. Knowing and using your competitive advantage wisely in the marketplace can make the difference between innovation and growth, or decline. When it comes to identifying competitive advantage, leaders often ask questions that set them apart from their peers such as: what do *we* know how to do, that *they* do not; what resources or technologies do *we* have, that *they* do not; what do *we* understand about the market, that *they* do not; and what do our customers love about *us*, that they cannot find anywhere else? We can refer to questions like these as the search for competitive advantage in the form of *things*.

These are important questions; however, notice how none of them focus directly on the greatest asset that every organization possesses—the collective potential of people and their performance contributions. When I work with leaders and their teams to set their leadership and organization development goals, issues of competitive advantage invariably surface. When the theme arises, I surprise them with this question: *If you had no industry intelligence, no killer technology, no innovative production or service delivery model, no singular resource, and no brand loyalty that could push you ahead in the market—**who** would you rely on for our competitive advantage?* This hypothetical question wipes the slate clean and temporarily redirects people away from the obvious competitive advantages they may consider (i.e., stuff). We can refer to this question and others like it as the search for competitive advantage in the form of *people*.

Now, at this point reactions are often positive and many people affirm the intent of the question with statements like: "Yes, of course, people are our most valuable asset." "We absolutely need to win in the talent wars." "We have to hire the best in order to get all of that potential innovation and next-generation potential through our doors—and keep it away from our challengers." While statements like these may ring true, if you ask people what they need in their talent, there is very little consensus on what would truly deliver a competitive advantage.

Most people restate the tried and true leadership dimensions that have survived the test of time. They may say that we need people who are honest, committed, focused on our mission, on-board with the team, and willing to do the little things it takes to succeed. Still others may refer to the more popular, recent assessments of skills for the new millennium by saying we need our people to be change-minded, capable of synthesizing complex ideas, right-brain thinkers with a penchant for innovation, self-starters who can identify challenges and opportunities without being told, tech-savvy individuals who can leverage new technology channels for virtual work, and outstanding contributors with capabilities that can be adapted in flexible ways as our needs change, and so on. Both of these lists are useful, and I would agree that all of these qualities matter in some way. But if everybody knows they matter and recruits accordingly, there really is no competitive advantage in them.

I believe that one of the most significant competitive advantages for organizations in the twenty-first century is a workforce that has the capacity *to recognize the hidden curriculum of work and take deliberate steps to manage its demands.* To help people grasp this new definition of competitive advantage, I often introduce a follow-up scenario that can provoke more specific discussion about the power of *what people do* when they truly are an organization's competitive advantage:

> *You have to rebuild this organization from scratch. You do not have any of the typical competitive advantages you relied on in the past (i.e., no killer technology, promising research, etc.) and for the time being you can only work with the people you have right now. In this scenario, how would your people have to approach their work in order to create the necessary conditions for success?*

This question is critical because it forces you to think not about people and things at the surface level, but about what people do—specifically, what patterns of communication and interaction must exist at the foundation of the enterprise's success. I facilitated a discussion like this with two merging nonprofit leadership teams. The executive directors and pivotal board members from both organizations were present, and the question was relevant because the merger would literally *rebuild a new organization* from the best of both existing agencies.

As they moved through the discussion, they were able to pinpoint critical themes within their responses to the prompt. The group shared comments such as (a)"People will need to communicate honestly about issues, without fear of being seen as part of the old guard. While there should be some pressure to let go of old ways, we have to remember that many of the old ways worked" and (b) "The interactions of leaders need to be focused less on the tasks, activities, and administrative challenges of the merger, but on ways people interact and make new habits. If there are clear roles, then those interactions should complement each other." As the session progressed, these kinds of concrete statements began to surface the key elements of their challenges and provided sufficient resources to draw upon for a successful merger.

Make no mistake about it, every competitive advantage should be captured and leveraged to its fullest. If there are technology breakthroughs, innovations in production, marketing strategies, recruitment and selection improvements, or any other people/things that can help the organization succeed, they should be put in play. That said, any discussion about these perceived competitive advantages will be more effective if it includes the third domain described above: *a commitment to intentionally revealing and navigating the hidden curriculum of work,* which is the foundation of individual, team, and organizational success.

KEY TAKEAWAYS

In this post-average economy, those who know how to reveal opportunities for improved learning and performance will meet the challenge of change, stay relevant at work, and give themselves the best chance for long, successful working lives. Organizations that are filled with Future-Proof leaders and teams—those who create systems that increase the capacity of their people to transform the hidden challenges of work into opportunities for improved learning and performance—will win in the market. Gaining this competitive advantage begins with individual responsibility. Now, unlike any time in the past, your own ongoing employability comes from your capacity to independently and consistently add increasing value to the organization, not simply from your title or tenure in the organization as it may have been in the past.

Because the complexity and pace of change in the modern world of work show no signs of letting up, the three typical response patterns to work—sticking your Head in the Sand, Brute Force, and Calvary Calls—only threaten to make us fall farther behind. Cleaning out this bottleneck with a new approach resolves the inverse equation of *less available time and energy for the things that require more focused effort,* which so often leaves people feeling buried and overwhelmed. Seeing the hidden curriculum of work up close is the only way to take these first, necessary steps and capitalize on one of the greatest potential competitive advantages of the twenty-first century.

Chapter 4

GET YOUR WORKING LIFE R-I-T-E

YOU NOW HAVE A COMPLETE background and understanding about the myth of your working life, the need for a new approach to work, and the specific ways in which the changing conditions of work make it an urgent responsibility to go beyond your job description to address the hidden curriculum of work. In this environment where average is over and the fast, changing, and relentless pace of work makes it increasingly hard to find your way through the hidden challenges of work, you need a compass.

A compass is a navigational instrument that allows you to measure direction in a frame of reference relative to your surroundings. From this frame of reference you can discern the cardinal directions that orient you to where you are and where you are potentially heading. In the same way, the R-I-T-E Model provides an orientation to the true challenges and opportunities within your hidden curriculum of work.

To navigate the challenges along your path to *breakthrough performance*, your compass is the *R-I-T-E Model*, which is a series of progressive steps, including:

Reveal Your Hidden Curriculum of Work
   Vital Purpose + Valued Contributions + Barriers = Your "Job-within-the-Job"
Identify Barriers That Mark Pathways to Learning and Performance
   The everyday, core challenges that prevent you from doing your best work
Transform Barriers and Navigate Your Hidden Path to Success at Work
   Nav-Maps that resolve challenges and keep you on purpose contributing your best

Establish Future-Proof Plans for Yourself, Your Team, and Your Organization
  A specific plan to manage the hidden side of work

Once you become aware of the hidden curriculum of work, the R-I-T-E Model offers the milestones that you can use to go from remaking your own working life to creating an organizational culture that is full of Future-Proof leaders and teams. Each stage is important by itself, but when taken together, the overall progression can be transformative.

At the front end, it starts with *Revealing Your Hidden Curriculum of Work*. The opportunity here is to change the way you think about work by shifting away from the SMW to full acknowledgment that the hidden curriculum of work exists. This shift takes you from deficit thinking about the demands of work to a constructive mind-set that encourages you to see your vital purpose and value-added contributions as tools to meet the ongoing challenges of your working life. The primary tools necessary for this stage include the Six-Question Matrix and the Barriers to Learning and Performance Assessment (BLPA) described in chapter 5.

The heart of R-I-T-E Model—*Identifying Barriers That Mark Pathways to Learning and Performance* and *Transforming Barriers and Navigating Your Hidden Path to Success at Work*—is where the most significant change can happen. These steps help you understand your specific barriers and use a visual process to transform them into pathways toward something better. This is not hyperbole; with a little bit of process there is a way to leverage your hidden challenges at work into stepping stones to improve the quality of your working life. A vivid picture of your barriers defined and transformed is called a *Nav-Map*, and you will learn to draw them in chapter 6.

On the backend, the progression comes full-circle as you focus on *Establishing Future-Proof Plans for Yourself, Your Team, and Your Organization*. The goal here is to integrate the positive results from your individual process and use those to make lasting changes that affect other levels of leadership, and ultimately the entire culture of the organization.

The R-I-T-E Model is not a prescriptive formula that you have to follow; it is a way of thinking about the critical choice points you encounter in the world of work. Whether you think of it as a compass, a game plan, or just a reference point, each phase of the sequence will increase your capacity to successfully meet the goals you have for your working life. The remainder of this book brings the R-I-T-E Model to life and provides a mix of both knowledge and practice-guides to help you use this *compass* to your greatest advantage.

KEY TAKEAWAYS

In an environment where average is over and the fast-moving, relentless pace of change makes it increasingly hard to find your way through the hidden challenges of work, you need a compass. To navigate the challenges along your path to *breakthrough performance* your compass is the *R-I-T-E Model.* The four progressive stages of the model allow you to *Reveal Your Hidden Curriculum of Work, Identify Barriers That Mark Pathways to Learning and Performance, Transform Barriers and Navigate Your Hidden Path to Success at Work,* and *Establish Future-Proof Plans for Yourself, Your Team, and Your Organization.* With a mix of related insights, guided coaching activities, and hands-on exercises, the R-I-T-E Model offers a reorientation to the true demands of work and it delivers a lifeline for people who need to stand out and stay ahead.

Chapter 5

SEEING YOUR
"JOB-WITHIN-THE-JOB"

BEGINNING WITH THE FIRST PART of the R-I-T-E Model, part 2 of this book is designed to help you *Reveal Your Hidden Curriculum of Work*. This revelatory process will likely change the way you think about and approach your career from this point forward. Once you see the true nature of your "job-within-the-job," you will have a new level of awareness about the true demands of work and the opportunities they present. This new awareness marks the starting place along your path to success at work, and it holds the key to a long, successful working life.

The process of revealing your hidden curriculum of work will be completed in two parts. First, you will explore the inner dimensions of your "job-within-the-job," including its vital purpose, greatest value, and all of the hidden challenges that make it hard for you to get your best work done. A series of questions and interactive prompts will help you glimpse a true picture of your working life. Once the full-scope of your "job-within-the-job" is clear, I will help you to identify the specific barriers that reduce your performance and erode the quality of your working life. These two elements—seeing the value that you can add above and beyond your standard job description *and* recognizing the barriers to learning and performance that threaten your success—will frame the precise picture of your hidden curriculum of work. Your path to getting beyond the job description and achieving *breakthrough performance* runs right through both of them.

Between these two pivotal steps I will lead you through an exercise to put your hidden curriculum of work in *Three Dimensions*. This focused activity explores the ways in which both your "job-within-the-job" and the everyday barriers to learning and performance impact others. The outcome is a relationship map that you can use to more effectively partner with others as you navigate your hidden curriculum of work.

All of the related activities in part 2 have been used with great effect in many individual, team, and organizational contexts, and you will have the opportunity to work through them at an accelerated pace. However, I have to warn you upfront: the process of seeing the true nature of work for the first time may result in an interesting mix of feelings. Surprise is not exactly the right word to describe what happens. I actually had to coin my own term to help people adjust to the experience: *duhprise*.

> *duh·prise* – noun/1: the moment you see your hidden curriculum of work clearly and realize you just revealed something you have always known, but never seen; 2: the mixed feeling of duh + surprise

SIX-QUESTION MATRIX

After years of working with clients to uncover and resolve the many challenges posed by the hidden curriculum of work, I developed a framework of six sequential questions that initiate the heavy lifting of this process. Just like an innovative technology company sells you features for your phone and tablet that you didn't even know you needed, the Six-Question Matrix helps you solve problems that you didn't even know you had. Together, the questions take the superficial side of work that we already know about and then integrate it with the hidden elements of the "job-within-the-job." This process lays the groundwork for identifying the challenges and obstacles that have prevented you from achieving success in your job. The six questions include:

1. *What Single Statement Best Describes Your Role?*
2. *What Tasks and Activities Absorb Most of Your Time?*
3. *What Are the Greatest Challenges That Prevent Your Best Work?*
4. *What Single Statement Reveals Your Vital Purpose to the Organization?*
5. *Which of Your Contributions Have the Greatest Value to the Organization?*
6. *What Are the Hidden Challenges of Delivering This Value?*

Questions 1–3 reflect the SMW. These first prompts are easier to respond to because they are the "stuff of work" that you know and deal with on a daily basis. Questions 3–6 mark a shift toward the hidden side of work. Question 4 is a deeper reframe of question 1, and question 6 draws out the initial response from question 3.

Here is an example that illustrates the process of working through the six questions. Several years ago I worked with the CTO of a small technology company who hired me to help work through the daily struggle of *playing constant catch up* and *failing to get ahead of the short-term challenges enough to address long-range issues.* I went through each level to expose his hidden curriculum of work, beginning with the role statement reflected in his formal job description:

1. *What Single Statement Best Describes Your Role?*
   "I'm the CTO…My job is to make sure our technology needs are met so that our business units function to their full potential."
2. *What Tasks and Activities Absorb Most of Your Time?*
   - Attending lots of meetings.
   - Sending lots of e-mails to make sure everyone is on the same page.
   - Putting out fires and responding to emergencies when there are crashes in the system.
3. *What Are the Greatest Challenges That Prevent Your Best Work?*
   - Constantly playing catch up.
   - Reacting to emergencies, not proactively moving forward on goals.
   - Shifting priorities and the continuously changing technology platforms that make our goals a "moving target."
4. *What Single Statement Reveals Your Vital Purpose to the Organization?*
   "I anticipate the needs of our business units and try to identify feasible technology solutions that will meet them. If I can do this well, before they even

realize they have a need, then that is priceless. Anytime our technology solutions respond to real needs that help people do their jobs better, there is less resistance to implementation and our entire operational performance gets a boost."

5. *Which of Your Contributions Have the Greatest Value to the Organization?*
   - I make sure people understand the importance of creative discussions and scenario exercises that put us in the "future-state" and help predict how our needs may change.
   - I persuade our business partners and unit leaders to understand the balance between meeting their specific needs and addressing the company's overall needs.
   - I get buy-in from the CEO to invest significant resources in technology solutions that (in some cases) have long lead times and high risk, but also big pay-offs if they keep us ahead of the game.
   - I set the tone for my team based on my focus and what I raise hell about; they follow my example.

6. *What Are the Hidden Challenges of Delivering This Value?*
   - People are often so wrapped up in their everyday stuff they don't see the value of long-range planning. They also sometimes get the wrong idea and think that we are planning to change things that are working well.
   - Our business unit leaders are really top-notch, as a result they advocate pretty effectively for their needs. I really want to accommodate them, so it is hard to draw a line and say "no" when there is an organizational priority that trumps a departmental need. I struggle to know the difference at times, and when they see my confidence waiver, they wear me down.
   - Anytime I recommend a technology platform I realize I am putting my career on the line; if I guess wrong it could costs us millions. The CEO trusts me and I have to maintain that trust. At the same time, I can't be afraid to disagree and work through opinions that are different from mine in order to get to the *right answer*.
   - When I react, they react. I have to moderate my own stress level and avoid getting caught up in the crisis of the day. I have to motivate my team to take the long view as well, but they also can't take their eyes off the prize, which is customer-driven responsiveness.

Upon completing this exercise with the young CTO, the first thing he said was, "Wow, there *are* two very different roles here!" I simply looked at him and said, "Bingo, this is part of the reason why things have felt so overwhelming for you." His immediate and honest reaction was the *duhprise* moment I was hoping for because it shifted his perspective in a profound way.

After finishing this exercise, he quickly began to rethink many aspects of his approach to work, including managing his key relationships where there was little knowledge about his vital purpose, valued contributions, and genuine challenges. More than anything, the experience of seeing a more comprehensive picture of his world of work seemed to restore his energy and motivation to keep charging ahead.

Here is another example of the six questions presented in the form of a matrix, which organizes the response in two levels and shows how question 4 is truly *the* significant turning point in the process.

I worked with a new regional manager at a public agency whose mission was to provide social services to youth and families. The director of the agency hired me to help with the transition because the previous regional manager had exited the organization with a lot of hurt feelings. After two months on the job, things were not going as well as she wanted, so I began to coach her to achieve goals related to increasing the engagement and morale of team members, holding people accountable for new processes and expectations, and developing positive relationships with direct reports while also leading some tough changes. At one of our early sessions, I led her through each level of the questions to expose her "job-within-the-job." Table 5.1 demonstrates the results of her Six-Question Matrix with dotted-lines (around question 4) to highlight the transition point to the hidden side of work.

This Six-Question Matrix produced a big "ah-ha moment" for my client. For her, a major takeaway was the way in which her vital purpose and core contributions were *invisible*. She could not recall having a single conversation (with her boss, with peers, or with any direct reports) where these things were openly discussed. To help solidify the point, I asked a rhetorical follow-up question to gauge her response: "So, you're telling me that the most important things you are doing for your team and the agency are things that: (A) You don't talk about with anyone else; (B) You're not being evaluated on or held accountable for; and (C) They are not even in your job description?" Welcome to the hidden curriculum of work.

Table 5.1 Completed Six-Question Matrix

1. What Single Statement Best Describes Your Role? "I'm the regional manager…My job is to make sure our case managers follow policies and procedures and meet the needs of our consumers."	

2. **What Tasks and Activities Absorb Most of Your Time?**	3. **What Are the Greatest Challenges that Prevent Your Best Work?**
• Reviewing case files and outcome reports • Attending triage meetings with staff and addressing concerns with families • Trying to keep everyone happy and motivated, despite how overwhelmed people feel	• Everyone is under a ton of pressure (including me) and we've been doing the work of multiple people since the last round of budget cuts and hiring freezes • My style is pretty direct and sometimes people need more encouragement and support than I'm willing to give • There are very few direct conversations where people seem willing to say what is on their mind

4. What Single Statement Reveals Your Vital Purpose to the Organization?
"I'm the last line of defense as far as making sure we do the right thing by both state policy and by our consumers. I might catch a major error that could result in a grievance or something embarrassing, so I have to be vigilant about the decisions our case managers make. My ability to educate staff about how to effectively make choices is a direct reflection of both our compliance and the quality of service our consumers receive."

5. **Which of Your Contributions Have the Greatest Value to the Organization?**	6. **What Are the Hidden Challenges of Delivering This Value?**
• I educate people about how to handle those gray areas when 2+2 = anything but 4 • I keep the peace by showing support for our case managers' decisions, but also supporting our consumers' needs • I translate what our director wants to see happen with what is actually possible	• Many of the case managers were hired based on their ability to follow rules, which can get in the way of the flexible thinking needed to solve problems for our families • There is such a strong sense of loyalty among staff that they interpret supportive things I say to families as a breach of trust and failure to support their decisions

Table 5.1   Continued

• I have a fresh, objective perspective that can cut through the clutter of how things used to be	• I don't always feel like our senior leaders are on the same page. So often something that is announced one day is revoked the next, which causes uncertainty and jades people • People assume I don't know things because I am unwilling to just "do what's always been done"—I'm actually trying to change the culture, but people can be close-minded

Another breakthrough for her was the contradiction she exposed by noting that *many of the case managers were hired based on their ability to follow rules,* which can get in the way of *the flexible thinking needed to solve families' dynamic problems.* This brought the tension between compliance and flexible problem solving into a much clearer focus for her. Overall, noticing the inherent paradox between the job and the "job-within-the-job" informed how she planned to recruit and manage staff differently in the future. The process also brought her greater peace of mind when she put her finger on the culture-change issue she consistently bumped up against. One of the core contributions she recognized in her role was the *fresh, objective perspective that can cut through the clutter of how things used to be.* In a culture where people often cling to past ways of thinking and acting, this was an important driver to push back against the unwillingness to change and the mind-set of just "doing what's always been done."

Here is a final example that shows how an individual contributor, someone who had no management responsibilities, used the Six-Question Matrix. I worked with an operations coordinator at a Real Estate Management Group who was identified as a future high-potential leader. The founder and principal of the firm was considering him for a management position, but wanted to see improvement in a few areas. I was asked to help address growth areas related to effective communication in high-pressure situations, tracking details more closely to get the little things right, and being more comfortable saying "I don't know, but I'll get back to you" rather than overreaching with his job knowledge. During our first session, I led him through each level of questions to expose his hidden curriculum of work. Table 5.2 illustrates his responses within the matrix.

Table 5.2 Six-Question Matrix of a High-Potential Candidate

1. What Single Statement Best Describes Your Role? "I'm the low person on the organization chart, but I oversee all real-estate activities conducted by our firm's agents. Basically the agents do all the work, but they don't get paid until I sign off that their work was done right. This oversight protects the broker, my direct boss."	

2. What Tasks and Activities Absorb Most of Your Time?	**3. What Are the Greatest Challenges that Prevent Your Best Work?**
• Reviewing all the documents in each file and following up on missing or incomplete files • Staying up-to-date on each of our agents' current book of business and providing the necessary motivation to the agents to try and increase sales • Handling the marketing and promotional materials and ensuring that advertising opportunities are met	• Trying to support and motivate agents to follow through on details when they are technically independent contractors • Dealing with an undefined and often conflicting strategic course of business by the owner of the brokerage • Finding the time to educate myself on the new technological tools and regulatory changes and translating that new information for our agents

4. What Single Statement Reveals Your Vital Purpose to the Organization?
"The buck stops with me: I ensure that all of our agents comply with state regulations. I have to be the most efficient person in the company in order to keep the business continually churning to maximize the brokerage's profitability."

5. Which of Your Contributions Have the Greatest Value to the Organization?	**6. What Are the Hidden Challenges of Delivering This Value?**
• Auditing all files accurately, eliminating possible liability issues for the agent and the brokerage • Keeping pace with timely audits files, which allows for agents' commissions to be paid quickly • Providing worthwhile tools, support, and motivation to our agents to increase business	• Every agent is different; finding methods to communicate and motivate each one effectively is tough • Writing company policies and procedures that will get followed by independent contractors with different levels of experience and ambition • Exposing various degrees of liability within each file that need to be dealt with in some way

During our follow-up conversation after the exercise, his wheels were really turning. He returned to his response to question 4 and noticed something really powerful about the fact that he had *to be the most efficient person in the company*. Reflecting on his training and orientation, he stated: "You would not think that this statement could be true considering the way I was brought on board...my training lasted two days and was filled with constant interruptions. I never really got a job description, and much of what I learned has been on the fly..."

This reflection allowed him to put a finger on a contradiction he felt day-in and day-out: as the low person on the organization chart, he had the least amount of time with senior brokers and he believed (perhaps assumed) that he was seen by others as less valuable. While he was treated very well, he recognized that there was less value placed upon his priorities, despite the fact that they were central to things running well (and for people to get paid). For example, when he followed up with people to track missing items down it often seemed like a nuisance, not like someone keeping a well-oiled machine rolling. Among other things, one of the action outcomes that resulted from this exercise was a commitment to finding subtle ways to create greater recognition for his vital contributions to the company, including requests for assistance from agents who made his job harder by their lack of follow-through on key tasks.

Now that you have seen a few examples, it is time for you to complete your own Six-Question Matrix. You do not need to look for a major insight or some kind of "ah-ha moment." You are simply lifting the curtain and taking look at the scene it reveals. This subtle look holds the potential for changing the way you approach your work. Sometimes the small insights can result in the greatest change.

SELF-GUIDED SIX-QUESTION MATRIX

Questions 1, 2, and 3 pertain to the SMW—your known world of work. Your job was designed by those rules, you have been managed according to those rules, and it is the reliance on those rules that likely prevents you from focusing on the stuff below the dotted line (questions 4, 5, and 6). The final two questions reveal your greatest value to the organization (what will make you Future-Proof) and your true challenges (the barriers that you must resolve). This activity is the opening move to start navigating your hidden curriculum of work and uncovering your hidden path to success. Using the prompts in table 5.3, reveal your own "job-within-the-job."

Table 5.3   Self-Guided Six-Question Matrix

1. *What Single Statement Best Describes Your Role?*	
2. *What Tasks and Activities Absorb Most of Your Time?*	**3. *What Are the Greatest Challenges that Prevent Your Best Work?***
4. *What Single Statement Reveals Your Vital Purpose to the Organization?*	
5. *Which of Your Contributions Have the Greatest Value to the Organization?*	**6. *What Are the Hidden Challenges of Delivering This Value?***

Before moving to the next step, it can be helpful to reflect on this process and focus attention on things that may be different for you, moving forward, by considering the following questions:

- Looking at your answers, which response is the most unexpected to you, and which one is the most predictable?
- What is the contrast between the tasks/activities you are responsible for (question 1) and the vital purpose to the organization (question 4)?
- Specifically, in what ways does your vital purpose potentially match or not match what people think your role is?
- If you showed your responses to the six questions to others in the organization, would they be surprised? If so, which questions do you think would be most interesting to them?
- How consistently do you feel you can deliver the valued contributions to the team/organization at the level you want?
- When it comes to the hidden challenges you identified (question 6), which ones are the most difficult to address?

- What do you need in the form of resources and support to resolve these challenges?
- Who else needs to know about your responses to these six questions?
- Overall, what has the impact of this exercise meant to you?

THREE DIMENSIONS

The next major step in this process is to pinpoint the specific barriers to learning and performance that give your hidden curriculum of work its gritty character. However, before you can complete that step, you need to see the impact that your "job-within-the-job" has in three dimensions. The following exercise will show you just *how hidden* your true challenges at work are when you scan up, down, and across the organization. By putting them in three dimensions, you can better see the impact of your "job-within-the-job" on important people you work with.

Three examples of the Six-Question Matrix were provided in the previous section of this chapter. In those case studies we met the CTO of a technology company, a regional manager in a Social Services Agency, and an operations coordinator in a Real Estate Management Group. In each case, we learned about their "job-within-the-job" from a first-person perspective. Nobody is an island, and so it is important to assess the impact of the true challenges of work in three dimensions. The following exercise is a relationship-mapping activity that can help to pinpoint the necessary discussions and interactions that may be needed to address your challenges. Because well-crafted questions offer a powerful way to bring out elusive insights and understanding, I created this series of focused questions to help people assess the interfaces of their hidden curriculum of work.

At this point, you only need to be concerned with the most immediate collaborators at work, specifically those with whom you work most closely and who play a more direct role in your success on the job. For upward assessment, you want to consider your immediate supervisor and any other "bosses" that you may not report to directly, but who nonetheless have an impact on you. Start with the following questions:

1. *At this moment, how much does my boss know and understand about my "job-within-the-job"—including both the value that I contribute and the hidden challenges I face?*

2. *What do I need to communicate to make them aware of the true challenge of my work? How might they respond if I took time to share my perspective about it with them directly?*

3. *Am I held accountable for performance elements related to the true value I deliver, or just the standard tasks and activities I'm responsible for? What would shift in my relationship with my supervisor if I was managed based on this new picture of my true challenges at work?*

4. *Presently, is there support available to assist me in addressing the challenges that I encounter? What would change for me if I made more specific requests for it?*

As you can see, each of these questions makes the hidden curriculum of work visible, discussible, and malleable by you and others in the organization. One of the fundamental reasons that the hidden curriculum typically wreaks so much havoc on organizational life is precisely our inability to name it, talk about it in useful ways, and reshape it for our gain. While these questions do not *do the work*, they begin the process.

For lateral assessment with peers who are across from you on the organization chart, it helps to pick just two or three colleagues that are the most influential to your success. Whether you think of them as supporters or detractors, the goal here is to identify those that you interact with significantly and who play a role in your everyday challenges at work. For this dimension, answer these questions:

1. *Considering the individuals I interact with most frequently, how much do they know or understand about my "job-within-the-job"—including both the value that I contribute and the hidden challenges I face?*

2. *How much do I know or understand about the "job-within-the-job" of my key colleagues?*

3. *What would I need to communicate in order to make them aware of the true challenge of my work, as well as to learn more about theirs?*

4. *Overall, do these key players make it easier or more difficult for me to succeed in my "job-within-the-job"? In what ways?*

5. *Of the specific hidden challenges I have identified, which ones make it hard for me to collaborate and get great work done?*

6. *What steps could I take to improve our shared understanding about the impacts our challenges have on each other?*

These questions are truly just the tip of the iceberg. Wading into team dynamics and collaborative working relationships can suggest any number of angles to pursue with regard to what works well, what gets people stuck, and so on. However, the purpose of exploring this lateral dimension is to begin the process of thinking about your key interfaces in relation to what is unseen within your "job-within-the-job." I have always believed that peer relationships are much more significant than leaders give them credit for. While we know that one of the greatest influences on a person's success at work (and willingness to stay or leave an organization) is the quality of the relationship with their boss, it is the peer-based relationships at work that create the social system we rely on for support and connection.

Finally, it is time to complete the downward assessment. If you are in some kind of management function, it is critical that you reflect both on how much your people know about your own hidden curriculum of work, as well as on how much you know about the true challenges your direct reports face. If you have many formal direct reports, I suggest focusing initially on the pivotal ones you interact with most (i.e., those who you rely on for your own success at work more than others). The following questions move in both directions and can help you to understand the downward dimension:

1. *How well do I understand the "job-within-the-job" of my key reports?*
2. *How well do they understand their "job-within-the-job"—including both the value that they contribute and the hidden challenges they face?*
3. *What might change in their quality of performance and in our working relationships if I took the time to help them expose their hidden curriculum of work?*
4. *In what ways have I been hiring, managing, and evaluating based on the SMW, rather than on the realities of the hidden curriculum of work?*
5. *Do they understand my "job-within-the-job," including the various demands and pressures that impact how I work with them? What might shift if they gain a better understanding of and appreciation for these challenges?*
6. *If I completely altered my approach to managing others with full consideration of the hidden curriculum of work, what would likely be the most challenging part of that shift?*

Table 5.4 Bill's "Job-within-the-Job" in Three Dimensions

- My boss is a forward-thinking person, so I know that he would be interested in my effort to innovate in my approach to leading the technology function in the company
- He hates excuses, so what's good about the Six-Question Matrix is that the emphasis is not on finding someone or something to blame. Instead it looks at what individuals can do to close their performance gaps
- I am planning to show him how I plan to make changes in our division (i.e., recruiting and selecting staff based on the true demands of our work) then I'll see if it makes sense to roll this out company-wide

Up

• The C-level leaders definitely do not know about my hidden challenges, nor am I familiar with theirs • A lot of the assumptions I have been making are based on such generic ideas about what they do for the company—I really want to dig deeper into this. We could likely learn from each other	**Across**	• Communicating with them about the idea of the hidden curriculum of work would be well received because they all want better performance; this points toward some of the gaps • When we make our reports to the CEO it is always based on these quarterly numbers that just don't tell the story about the challenge of running a great business

Down

- My key reports don't fully understand the challenges I face in my role, and I don't understand theirs either
- The need to anticipate is so important, but I think that people hesitate to act because of the risk involved
- If I helped them to tease our their "job-within-the-job," I think I would see some valuable contributions that I'm not even aware of
- My people are probably doing a lot of things right, but I just don't know about them because they are taken for granted
- I think that our division can recruit and select better by re-designing our technical interviews around the "job-within-the-job"

BILL'S THREE DIMENSIONS

To provide a clear example of what it means to put your "job-within-the-job" in three dimensions, in table 5.4 illustrates the work that Bill, the rising CTO, did to see his hidden curriculum of work at the pivotal intersections of his working relationships.

If you look carefully at Bill's Three Dimensions, you can see that he pinpointed some really important features, from personal changes like communicating more directly with his CEO, to systemic changes like reworking the interview process for technical positions. While the final version of his three-dimension grid did not respond to every question, it summarizes the main points at all three levels.

With Bill's example as a guide, it is now time for you to put your own "job-within-the-job" in Three Dimensions. Using the blank template in table 5.5, scan your vital relationships up, down, and across and consider ways to understand how you can integrate your hidden curriculum of work more effectively.

Table 5.5 Self-Guided Exercise: Putting Your "Job-within-the-Job" in Three Dimensions

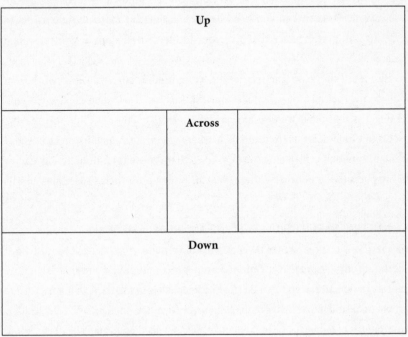

HIDDEN CHALLENGES IN YOUR "JOB-WITHIN-THE-JOB"

Now that you can see what your "job-within-the-job" is all about, including the various ways it shows up in all Three Dimensions of your work experience, you have revealed a significant part of your hidden curriculum of work. This brings us to the last and most important exercise. You need to pinpoint the precise barriers to learning and performance that make it hard for you to get your best work done. This is about taking your initial response to question 6 in your Six-Question Matrix to a deeper level. Accurately identifying the core barriers you face at this stage will put you directly on the path to improved learning and performance. This is what will make you future-proof and give you the best chance to take control of your working life and gain leverage to change the things that produce unwanted experience and outcomes for you on the job.

The remainder of this chapter provides a summary of barriers and it introduces the Barriers to Learning and Performance Assessment (BLPA) that you can self-administer to spot some of your core challenges. I created this research-based assessment tool to help people gain a better vantage point on their hidden curriculum of work. The short version is something you can take right now; the full 40-statement version can be found in appendix 1. Before you take the assessment, you need to know a little bit more about barriers to learning and performance that give your hidden curriculum of work so much "character."

By identifying core barriers within your hidden curriculum of work, you can gain a measure of influence that the increased awareness can give you. The fact is that what we are unaware of controls us. By revealing the specific facets of our hidden curriculum of work, we begin to notice its pressures and demands, which can free us to respond to them more intentionally. Instead of being perpetually bound by them, we can understand their causes and conditions and transform them.

IDENTIFYING BARRIERS TO LEARNING AND PERFORMANCE

As the Six-Question Matrix reveals, each of us has a vital purpose to fulfil, and there are things that we contribute to our team and organization that are highly valued. In question 6 you named the hidden challenges that make it hard to stay on purpose and deliver this value. Whatever form the challenges of our hidden curriculum of work arrive in, collectively I refer to them as *barriers to learning and performance*. Although we may have skills and resources to address some of them, these issues and challenges represent the murky half of our hidden curriculum of work and they often go unresolved.

> I define a *barrier* to workplace learning and performance as: *any expressed behavior, attitude, or action that distracts, impedes, or prevents individual, team, or organizational learning and performance.*

If you have not already completed the Six-Question Matrix you can begin right now with a few simple questions: What challenges am I experiencing at work? What problems are they creating in my working life? And, what might be causing and sustaining the core issue in play?

Notice the focus of the question: *what,* not *who.* "Who" is not the focus of the question, because a focus on "who" leads to attribution/blame on others, and conversely, can result in a lack of ownership for addressing things on our part. It is true that we all have blind spots, which are those performance gaps that we sustain in part because we just cannot see them. By avoiding the "who" questions for the time being we avoid the potential risk of avoiding full accountability for our own contributions to the challenge at hand.

There is a time and a place for understanding the "who," but Future-Proof thinkers don't care much about it. Future-Proof thinkers want to get to the core barrier fast in order to transform it efficiently. In most cases the answer to the question "Who is responsible for causing a headache" is *us* (at least in part), so it proves to be a waste of time distinguishing a person or part of the system early on. What is important is our ability to stay objective and to use that relative distance to see things as they are, for what they are, so that we can get down to the business of generating new outcomes.

Here are a few common barriers that you may encounter in the workplace. The "Everyday Barriers" should look familiar to you, while some of the "Elusive Barriers" listed below may seem new. In an effort to reflect the realities of everyday working life, they are described in plain language. Which ones have caused challenges for you?

EVERYDAY BARRIERS

Everyday barriers show up in offices, cubicles, and meeting rooms in the world of work. We may all refer to them with different names, but once we've experienced them, we can see them coming from a mile away and they are a surefire way to end up at impasse with the hidden curriculum of work! Common examples include:

- Our communication breaks down
- Change fatigue! People are burning out
- We're tripping over each other (no clear goals/roles)
- People are afraid to speak up and share their perspectives
- Our culture is too competitive and teamwork suffers
- We give and give…but there's no connection between performance and reward
- Our managers don't walk their talk
- There are too many difficult personalities around here
- There's too much talk about "how it used to be" and not enough innovation

ELUSIVE BARRIERS

These are also common barriers that show up in offices, cubicles, and meeting rooms in the world of work; however, they are often hidden just below the surface. In addition to being harder to identify, they can also be tough to define. Again, we may refer to them with different names, but when they show up our learning and performance decline!

- Accomplishing lesser priorities well while failing to focus on top goals
- Anxiety, distraction, or avoidance from information overload
- Attempting to implement new behaviors without changing the old system in place
- Addressing only superficial issues without solving root causes/problems
- An organizational culture that enables polarized views and split alliances
- Failure to follow through and commit to action
- Greater challenges than available energy/resources to meet them
- Inability to let go of past ways of thinking or acting
- Failure to bounce back from adversity
- Inflexible expectations that do not encourage innovation or accept mistakes
- The presence of unresolved conflict that reduces communication
- Too much complacency and not enough urgency to make necessary change
- Treating all goals and outcomes the same and missing critical priorities

Barriers such as these matter because whenever obstacles to learning and performance are present for us, we experience disruptions in individual/team productivity that eventually hurt the organization's bottom line. Conversely, progress and positive development occur for us when barriers to performance are eliminated. You can read more about the science behind these barriers in appendix 3, but for now let's get back to the heart of the matter: **the barriers within our hidden curriculum of work cause major challenges to our performance and erode the quality of our working lives.**

THE DAMAGING EFFECTS OF UNRESOLVED BARRIERS

The damaging effects of unresolved barriers produce effects on the quality of our learning and performance at three levels, including:

1st-Tier Effects on Individuals

The presence of unresolved barriers can cause individuals to lose focus, stop collaborating with others, avoid priorities, decrease motivation, produce lower-quality work, cause physical and psychological discomfort through stress, and disengage from their work and the organization.

2nd-Tier Effects on Teams

The presence of unresolved barriers can debilitate team communication, prevent effective decision making, reduce collaboration, erode morale, distract from priorities and goals, and undermine the collective potential of the individuals on a given team to make a positive impact on the larger organization.

3rd-Tier Effects on Organizations

The organization is the sum of all of its individuals. With unresolved barriers, individual and team productivity decline, dysfunctional patterns of communication and interaction increase, and the effects of these things in the form of ineffective collaboration and decision making can crush the bottom line. The presence of unresolved barriers also increases the intensity and volume of gripes, which sour workplace culture, hurt morale and engagement, and ultimately increase turnover.

BARRIERS MARK THE HIDDEN PATH TO SUCCESS AT WORK

Although barriers are everywhere, all the time, the good news is that when identified and understood accurately from all relevant perspectives, *barriers mark the pathways to improved learning and performance.* They are signposts on our hidden path to success at work that point us toward the needed changes in our thinking and behavior that—if made—will result in greater success for us through improved learning and performance. This is what learning to navigate the hidden curriculum of work in part 3 will teach you. It is a framework that can be used to navigate some of the most subjective, complex dilemmas faced in the workplace. It casts a brighter light on the obstacles that adversely impact our learning and performance, which can subsequently be transformed into negotiable pathways for positive change and growth. However, before learning that system, it is important to stay focused on identifying the true, core barrier you are dealing with.

There is an old adage that a problem properly defined is half-solved. If this is true, then a barrier fully observed is partially dissolved. This implies the critical importance of accurately identifying barriers. Despite the elusiveness of barriers and the fact that they are often hidden in plain sight, barriers *can be* identified and understood comprehensively. In many cases, individuals and teams often have a fuzzy awareness of the superficial, presenting barriers or issues that they experience. As a result the meaning we give them is also limited. This kind of limited perspective makes it difficult to see barriers for what they are and to address them substantively.

There is only one rule when identifying your core barriers: they cannot start with the phrase "lack of ____." This is a lazy way of avoiding the more important, but admittedly harder, work of precisely naming the true gap. Lack of skills…lack of training…lack of motivation…lack of incentives…while these statements could be true, they are really not helpful descriptions of barriers when you think about them. Instead of pointing to the "lack," dig deeper to identify what is needed, then frame it accordingly. Lack of skills, for example, could really be about the *inability to secure technical training necessary to excel in a specific task*. Lack of motivation could be framed as *the inability to draw on enough energy to meet goals*, or *other things just matter more*. And, the lack of incentives is perhaps more about an *unwillingness to work as hard as needed because the reward is not valued*. Understood in this way, the *lack of* becomes helpful.

BARRIERS TO LEARNING AND PERFORMANCE ASSESSMENT

To assist you in the recognition of barriers to learning and performance that populate your hidden curriculum of work, Table 5.6 provides an abbreviated version of the BLPA[1] that will help you get on track. To complete the assessment, read each statement below and then rank it according to "frequency" and "impact" with a 1, 2, 3 or 4, depending upon how often you observe the

Table 5.6 The 10-Statement BLPA

Frequency Ratings	Impact Ratings
1 = I *Rarely* experience this barrier in the workplace.	1 = When I experience this barrier the impact is **insignificant and negligible.**
2 = I *Sometimes* experience this barrier in the workplace.	2 = When I experience this barrier the impact is **noticeable and bothersome**.
3 = I *Often* experience this barrier in the workplace.	3 = When I experience this barrier the impact is **obvious and challenging**.
4 = I *Frequently* experience this barrier in the workplace.	4 = When I experience this barrier the impact is **unavoidable and destructive**.

Description of Learning & Performance Barriers	Frequency	Impact
Absence of dialogue and limited expression of diverse viewpoints	1 2 3 4	1 2 3 4
Accomplishing lesser priorities well while failing to focus on more important objectives	1 2 3 4	1 2 3 4
Lack of reflection and learning from past successes and failures	1 2 3 4	1 2 3 4
Adopting novel, popular learning solutions that do not address specific and relevant organizational needs	1 2 3 4	1 2 3 4
An organizational culture in which individuals experience fear and distrust	1 2 3 4	1 2 3 4
Inability or unwillingness to adapt to fast-changing, complex, or uncertain conditions	1 2 3 4	1 2 3 4
Anxiety, distraction, or avoidance due to communication and information overload	1 2 3 4	1 2 3 4
Attempting to implement new behaviors and practices without changing the system that keeps old behaviors in place	1 2 3 4	1 2 3 4
Attributing successes to one's own abilities and efforts while blaming failures on other people or circumstances	1 2 3 4	1 2 3 4
Avoiding necessary learning due to short-term costs (i.e., time to attend sessions and implement new processes, etc.)	1 2 3 4	1 2 3 4

specific barrier during your experience at work and how impactful it is when experienced.

This assessment is instructive in two ways. First, it frames the importance of selecting barriers to focus on that are highly ranked in both dimensions of *frequency* and *impact*. Second, it names the typical root cause, or core barriers that are often just below the surface of the presenting conditions you face in your challenges at work.

In the space below, transfer the barriers you ranked with a combined score of 6–8 (feel free to rewrite them in your own words). You can also refer to your response to question 6 in the Six-Question Matrix for additional barriers to carry over. If none of the above barriers featured in the abbreviated BLPA match your current circumstances, write what you think the core barrier is (five words or less) and consider these three questions:

- Besides you, who is the one other person most affected by this and what is their relationship to you (e.g., coworker, boss, etc.)?
- How do you think the other person would describe the issue (ten words or less)?
- On a scale of 1–5, where "5" is extremely urgent and "1" is not urgent at all, how important is it to you to get this headache resolved?

These prompts are simply intended to start unpacking your barriers, so this is the pause point for the exercise. Part 3 of this book is dedicated entirely to understanding and resolving these barriers to help you successfully navigate the biggest challenges of your hidden curriculum of work.

WHY FOCUS ON THE NEGATIVE?

Now that you are knee-deep in barriers, it may be helpful to answer one last question: why focus on identifying something negative like barriers? Instead, why not take a more positive approach, like identifying what is being done well, and building on that? After all, strength-based approaches based on positive psychology research and intervention methods like Appreciative Inquiry[2] are popular and often effective. Someone recently asked me this very question because they wanted to know how, after all my years of working in professional development, coaching, and mediation—all of which are based upon the pursuit of strengths to build on toward positive solutions—why would I build a system is based on something negative like *barriers*.

The reason for this focus on barriers is because it offers the most efficient path toward constructive improvement. This is based upon an inherent assumption that identifying and potentially reducing barriers directly and indirectly improves the probability of successful workplace learning and performance. The primary foundation of this assumption comes from Kurt Lewin's force-field analysis.[3] Widely considered the "Father of Organization Development," Lewin worked extensively on issues of change in organizations. In his force-field analysis, you can either: (1) reduce the strength of the forces opposing a desired change (i.e., barriers); or (2) increase the forces that promote change so that both opposing forces are brought into balance. The system for resolving barriers that you will learn in part 3 actually works in both directions. It simultaneously reduces the impact of barriers by making the hidden curriculum of work visible, and it increases the positive force for change by transforming them into direct actions that can increase learning and performance over time.

In addition, I do not believe that barriers themselves are inherently negative. They are an inevitable aspect of our everyday working lives. When approached with a flexible attitude, barriers themselves can be the most powerful vehicles of learning. By reframing barriers as the pathway to learning and performance, we can elevate these formerly negative issues beyond the deficit thinking that casts them as something to avoid. This is a reframe that captures an important initial shift in thinking and draws our constructive attention toward barriers.

KEY TAKEAWAYS

Seeing your "job-within-the-job" is the first step required to reveal your hidden curriculum of work. Identifying your "job-within-the-job" can be done with the Six-Question Matrix, which is a series of prompts that converts the superficial side of your job into an honest picture of the true demands of your work. The new awareness you gain from seeing the hidden side of work marks the starting place along your path to success and it holds the key to a long, successful working life.

Once you complete the Six-Question Matrix, you can assess the impact your "job-within-the-job" has in Three Dimensions. Scanning up, down, and across the organization allows you to map the crucial relationships that influence your path to success. This step of putting your "job-within-the-job" in Three Dimensions allows you to grasp the impact it has on the important people you work with, including the steps you need to take to intentionally craft the mutually supportive relationships you need to better meet your challenges.

The final step in exposing the hidden curriculum of work is identifying the range of barriers that knock you off purpose, diminish your valued contributions, and get in the way of your best performance. Whenever these obstacles to learning and performance are present, they disrupt your productivity, which eventually hurts the organization's bottom line. Conversely, progress and positive development occur for us when barriers to performance are eliminated. When they are identified and understood accurately from all relevant perspectives, *barriers mark the pathways to improved learning and performance.* They are signposts on our hidden path to success at work that point us toward the needed changes in our thinking and behavior that—if made—will result in greater success for us through improved learning and performance.

Chapter 6

TRANSFORMING HIDDEN CHALLENGES WITH "NAV-MAPS"

YOU HAVE JUST REVEALED YOUR "job-within-the-job" and have come face-to-face with your hidden curriculum of work. Not only do you understand your vital purpose and the value-added contributions that can help you stand out and stay relevant on the job, you also have an emerging picture of the hidden challenges that can threaten your capacity to learn and perform well over time.

Now that you have learned how to see the hidden side of work, you will begin to notice that performance challenges exist everywhere, all the time. This is because our working lives are fertile places for these kinds of everyday issues and obstacles. Among other things, we work with difficult people, we operate in a state of constant change, our priorities shift, our goals get undermined by evolving circumstances, and we encounter unhealthy and destructive patterns of communication that cause misunderstanding, conflict, and stress.

The only effective way to truly deal with core issues is to face them head-on and address the root causes and conditions that create them. The next three chapters are devoted to showing you how to get down to this level and transform barriers to improve your learning and performance using Nav-Maps. At the conclusion of this chapter there is additional information about the rationale behind Nav-Maps, including why they are such an effective tool for navigating barriers. However, to get right into the process, here is a description of *Nav-Maps* (i.e., Navigation Maps), the primary tool you will use to resolve your everyday challenges at work.

NAV-MAP OVERVIEW

If encountering all kinds of barriers in your hidden curriculum of work is unavoidable, and if staying relevant at work requires that you overcome those barriers while finding ways to increase your learning and performance over time, then you need a process that can effectively and consistently meet these steep, diverse challenges. Nav-Maps are simple tools that illuminate the pitfalls and point the way toward better learning and performance.

The Nav-Map visually untangles the situation by assembling four interrelated elements that clarify the problem *and* the solution. Each of the four elements is helpful alone, but they are even more powerful together. Because it is a graphic tool, the Nav-Map allows you to rely on your visual capacity to understand a more comprehensive picture of individual or team learning and performance.

With Nav-Maps, what was abstract becomes concrete as multiple points of information and data are integrated in a set of four simple diagrams. A completed Nav-Map provides a snapshot of specific core learning and performance barriers, multiple perspectives on the causes and conditions of the issue, insight into the patterns that hold it in place, and a set of action steps and commitments required to transform it.

Using Nav-Maps allows you to explore very subjective perspectives with a level of objectivity that is required to see the full impact of performance gaps. The result is a single-page, data-rich, super graphic that provides a way of seeing patterns and relationships among variables that can be used to understand the hidden challenges of work and take meaningful action to resolve them.

Making Nav-Maps is a solution-focused process, but it is solution neutral insofar as the explicit outcomes are not pre-fixed. Your unique challenges

One size does not fit all; however core principles have a way of informing across contexts. Nav-Maps use a series of inter-related learning and performance processes that serve as effective tools for behavior change and developmental growth.

require equally original, customized solutions; therefore, the Nav-Map process channels your relevant information into the quality analysis and applicable decision tree that enables you to move forward.

To demonstrate this concept, figure 6.1 shows a completed Nav-Map. It may look somewhat complicated at first, but it is straightforward once you distinguish the relationship between the four parts. In this example, the core barrier is something that many people can relate to: "Change Fatigue." In this case, a small division within a larger financial services company was dealing with an onslaught of regulatory changes that kept everyone in constant "catch-up mode." The toll of the never-ending changes began to impact other aspects of the team's work. They created this Nav-Map to transform the root cause of the issue, which for them was framed as "too much change over a short period of time."

If you follow the Nav-Map from top-right in a clockwise direction, you see the full four-step progression required to resolve the core barrier. Each phase is described below in detail, including the concepts and process steps that went into creating the Nav-Map that helped the team move past the challenge and get their breakthrough.

NAV-MAP-MAKING TOOLS

Creating an accurate Nav-Map to successfully resolve barriers in your hidden curriculum of work requires four sequential components, including:

- Constellations;
- Varying Perspectives of Barriers (VPBs);
- Trip-Wire Patterns; and
- The Action Continuum.

CONSTELLATIONS OF BARRIERS

A Constellation is a pattern of related behaviors. Within a Constellation there is a core barrier at the center that holds other unwanted behaviors and outcomes in place. When you experience a constellation that you want to change,

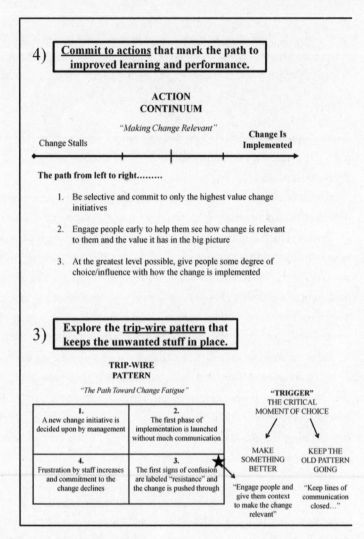

Figure 6.1   Completed Nav-Map.

remove the core barrier and the rest will naturally dissipate over time. The physics that hold behaviors and patterns of interaction in place are strong, so you have to get at the center for lasting change. Here are the basics of Constellations:

- Like points of light in the night sky, barriers to learning and performance cluster together around a core barrier that pushes and pulls other related barriers into relevance;

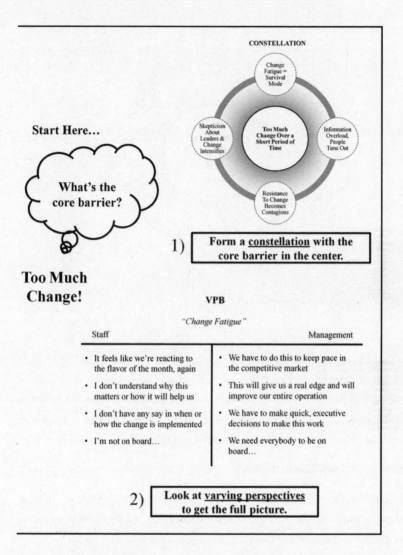

- This precise formation of interconnected barriers shows how the root cause or core barrier acts as the visible, predictive connector between related barriers;
- Constellations are tools for "untangling the entangled" because they allow barriers to be seen objectively as a pattern; and
- If you have experienced a particular core barrier, you will likely experience related satellite barriers. Conversely, if you resolve a core barrier, you potentially resolve its satellite barriers in the process.

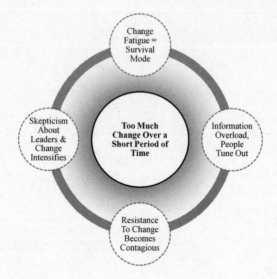

Figure 6.2   Constellation—Too Much Change.

If you attempt to change a Constellation by addressing only the satellite barriers, then the core will remain unchanged and no lasting shift can occur. The temporary relief may help, but the systemic habits of behavior are left in place. Figure 6.2 illustrates a sample Constellation from the Nav-Map, which shows how the core issue pushes and pulls the related behaviors into place.

How to Create a Constellation

1. For the individual(s) involved, use the BLPA or another tool to scan your work experience to identify the most commonly experienced barriers, or challenges at work.

2. Select the most interesting example of the identified barriers and subject it to the question, *"What is underneath this experience and what core issue seems to hold it in place?"* This allows you to look within the presenting description of the barrier to potentially see the core.

3. Place the most prominent, root-cause barrier in the center of the Constellation and explore additional questions such as: *What else does this barrier create* and *what seems to be pushed and pulled into your everyday experience because of it?*

4. Place these additional barriers in the peripheral circles.

5. Continue the process until the constellation is confirmed as accurate for the individual(s) involved.

VARYING PERSPECTIVES ON BARRIERS

Perspective shapes the way we understand ourselves and process our experience in the world of work. Individuals have a hard time seeing beyond their own viewpoints, which is what makes VPBs—a visual snapshot of Varying Perspectives of Barriers—so powerful. Here are the basics of VPBs:

- Our view of barriers is fluid, dynamic, and influenced by factors like our role, tenure, and power in an organization;
- By seeing with one perspective, we do not see from others;
- By expanding our own perspective we clarify a bigger picture by bringing more information into our field of view;
- Each unique vantage point is in some way accurate, but never absolutely complete;
- The grasp on a given vantage point proportionally distorts other vantage points; and
- Considering multiple, related perspectives can loosen and alter our original perspectives into something more dynamic.

Figure 6.3 provides an example from the Nav-Map that builds a deeper understanding of the impact from change-gone-bad. In this case, notice how different attitudes and behaviors shift depending upon the label of the role of each individual:

Staff	Management
• It feels like we're reacting to the flavor of the month, again	• We have to do this to keep pace in the competitive market
• I don't understand why this matters or how it will help us	• This will give us a real edge and will improve our entire operation
• I don't have any say in when or how the change is implemented	• We have to make quick, executive decisions to make this work
• I'm not on board...	• We need everybody to be on board...

Figure 6.3   VPB—Change Fatigue.

How to Create a VPB

1. Identify the individual(s) that are most affected by the core barrier captured in the Constellation and plot the people or perspectives across the "T-Bar." (This example shows two, but you can plot as many stakeholders or distinct perspectives you need to.)

2. Discuss how the issue is experienced, including the causes and conditions that sustain it and write down a few representative bullet points. The simple prompt here is: *"How do you see this issue playing out, and if you had to, what name would you give it?"*

3. Once all of the VPBs are highlighted and named, compare and contrast them in an objective way with questions like: *"What is similar and what is different about the way we see things? What happens when we single out just one of the perspectives and call it 'the right one' or the 'truth?' Now that there is a bigger picture here, in what ways might it be helpful to think differently about the varying perspectives?"*

Note: If you are working solo, use the same questions to create distinctions among your own varied perspectives. If others are involved, but for whatever reason, you cannot productively engage them in the Nav-Map making process, then you can guess their perspective. If this is the case, avoid the assumption that your guess is accurate and hatch a plan to get their input in the future. (For more information on team-based efforts, refer to chapter 13.)

TRIP-WIRE PATTERNS

Sometimes a core barrier and our reactions to it are "triggered" into effect and sustained by an all-too-familiar pattern of experience that acts as an unseen trip-wire to change. Our habits of communication and interaction often turn into *repeat reactions* that we rely on to respond to our recurring challenges and circumstances, whether they are helpful to us or not. Here are the basics of Trip-Wire Patterns:

- The causes and conditions that sustain barriers are often felt in the form of trip-wire patterns that distract us from the root causes of barriers;

- To transform barriers, you have to understand what keeps them in place, and then alter those conditions enough to disrupt the status quo;

- Drawing Trip-Wire Patterns allows you to map the attitudes/behaviors related to the core barrier and see how they are sustained;
- Trip-Wire Patterns have "trigger points" that activate the pattern and keep it in place. Triggers are a moment of critical choice to either: make something better, or resume the old pattern; and
- Triggers expose the "shoulds," "assumptions," and "knee-jerk reactions" that explain why we do what we do, even when we know it is unproductive.

The example from the Nav-Map in Figure 6.4 illustrates the Trip-Wire Pattern that ultimately created the change fatigue and prevented their effective change management as a result.

How to Identify a Trip-Wire Pattern

1. Create the "Trip-Wire" grid and identify the four elements that shape the pattern and hold the barrier in place.
2. Start looking for the key actions first, and then put each successive turn in "sequence" within the boxes (going clockwise from top-left).
3. Identify where the critical moment of choice is and put a star by it.
4. Answer the question, *"What would I/we need to do differently to shift the pattern to something different?"*
5. Contrast the two paths forward: the status quo that will keep the Trip-Wire Pattern in place, or the critical moment of choice to make something better.

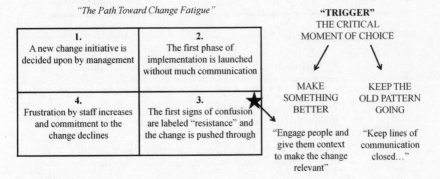

Figure 6.4   Trip-Wire Pattern—The Path Toward Change Fatigue.

ACTION CONTINUUM

You have to know where you are to know where you are going. The action continuum lets you plot your starting place in relation to the barrier you are dealing with, then set actions to move toward your goal of improved learning and performance. Here are the basics of an Action Continuum:

- Barriers mark the pathway to improved learning and performance;
- The resolution to the barrier lies within the barrier itself. If you turn the barrier inside out and stretch it, you find the pathway;
- The learning and performance element or goal is like a barrier in reverse. The continuum is the space between the push and pull of two equal, but opposing forces; and
- Drawing the continuum stirs the questions, *"Where am I right now?"* and *"What is required to begin moving from left to the right toward the goal?"*

Figure 6.5 displays the Action Continuum from the Nav-Map that shows a path toward a more effective response to the mandate for change.

How to Create an Action Continuum

1. Create a single line and place the core barrier from the Constellation on the left side of the continuum and its desired change—the inverse learning and performance aspiration—on the on the far right-side of the continuum.

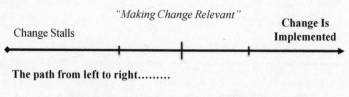

"Making Change Relevant"

Change Stalls

Change Is Implemented

The path from left to right.........

1. Be selective and commit to only the highest value change initiatives

2. Engage people early to help them see how change is relevant to them and the value it has in the big picture

3. At the greatest level possible, give people some degree of choice/influence with how the change is implemented

Figure 6.5   Action Continuum—Making Change Relevant.

2. Consider your current location as of "right now." If there are multiple individuals and/or differences of opinion about where things are at, simply take an average.

3. Using the critical moment to "shift the Trip-Wire Pattern," identify 2–4 key actions that will move you from experiencing the core barrier to something better.

Note: You are not looking to change everything overnight; you simply want a few carefully selected actions that can create movement. Start small and think about change incrementally.

UNPACKING NAV-MAPS: WHY VISUAL PROBLEM SOLVING WORKS

Now that you understand more about Nav-Maps and how to make them, this chapter concludes with a deeper explanation about why they can be so effective in the process of identifying and resolving everyday barriers to learning and performance.

We are all immersed in the hidden curriculum of work. Despite its often confusing and overwhelming effects, it is actually a data-rich environment. Information about our barriers to learning and performance is everywhere, and we are enmeshed in constant feedback loops regarding the attitudes and behaviors that move us toward our goals, or backfire and lead us astray. The problem is that most of this information is difficult to pinpoint and cumbersome to organize. This confusion makes it hard to take action on this information in meaningful ways. For example, consider one of the most challenging areas for all of us: working well with others.

Imagine that you are involved in a seemingly harmless conversation with a colleague, when it surprisingly goes sideways. Feelings get bruised and you are unclear as to what exactly caused the rift. If you are invested in the relationship then you will spend time doing "damage control" in order to figure out how to make it right and get the relationship back on track.

Understanding what exactly happened, why it occurred, and what immediate steps would rectify the situation requires an effective use of the information available to us. Nav-Maps provide a useful process of discovering and making productive use of this kind of complex (sometimes emotionally convoluted) information that is present, but often just out of our grasp.

Workplace relationships present the kinds of subjective, complex barriers that riddle the hidden curriculum of work. And despite the surprise and disappointment we experience when working relationships go bad, there is an abundance of critical information all around. However, that information is only as good as our ability to productively decode it.

In the big picture, the two primary goals of Nav-Maps are to: (1) Help you better manage the current events and challenges in your working life; and (2) Better predict what will likely occur in future situations so that you can create the preferred conditions where those problems occur less frequently (if at all) and with decreased impact.

Nav-Maps take information about your barriers from the hidden side of work, then add context. The result is a visual story about how core barriers to learning and performance affect the current state of your performance, and how they must be altered to affect the desired future state.

> "We should never forget that a picture of data is not the goal; it's only the means. Information visualization is all about gaining understanding so we can make good decisions."[1]

To overcome barriers to learning and performance, we have to turn weaknesses into strengths. Because our mental-processing system relies on selective perception (i.e., we apply cognitive filters that allow some details and information in, and not others) we have to learn how to see past our blind spots and biases that form resistance to seeing the patterns that hold our barriers in place. Nav-Maps create greater access to available information, and by visualizing the additional layers in the context of our actual experience, we see what we otherwise would not.

The diagrams and graphics built into Nav-Maps visually separate key pieces of information that can be used independently or together in sequence. These Nav-Maps give us a chance to make comparisons and to contrast themes, test for causality, and integrate contradictory vantage points in ways that help us deepen our understanding of the problem we face. As a gap-analysis tool for our learning and performance barriers, accurate Nav-Maps allow us to analyze the situation in objective ways so that we can solve problems in which we are simultaneously intertwined.

KEY TAKEAWAYS

Everyone—regardless of title and tenure in the organization—encounters a constant barrage of barriers in the hidden curriculum of work. Effectively identifying and resolving these unavoidable challenges is the key to staying relevant at work and increasing learning and performance over time. Nav-Maps, a visual process of organizing layers of subjective information about the causes and conditions of our performance challenges, are simple tools that illuminate the pitfalls and point the way toward better learning and performance. A well-drawn Nav-Map visually untangles the situation by assembling four interrelated elements that clarify the problem and lead to a practical solution. Creating an accurate Nav-Map starts with the four easy steps of drawing: Constellations, VPBs, Trip-Wire Patterns, and the Action Continuum. Each of the four progressions has value independently, but taken together they can be transformative.

Chapter 7

SUCCESS STORIES FROM THE HIDDEN SIDE OF WORK

I CONDUCTED THE RESEARCH, TESTED the concepts, refined the practices, and literally "wrote the book" on the hidden curriculum of work. However, the true teachers for me have been the countless leaders and organizational team members whose everyday experiences with the hidden side of work—and their willingness to trust me to work together on solving them—marked the way. The purpose of this chapter is to share some of those everyday experiences from people who peeled back the layers of their hidden curriculum of work and successfully used the R-I-T-E Model to get their *breakthrough*.

The following case examples show three different configurations of the tools you have just learned. They are written in a straightforward way to give you simple ideas for navigating your own challenges at work. In addition to the diversity of content within the examples, there is also diversity of delivery. The final case was facilitated by a consultant, while the first two were self-directed by the participants themselves. This mix illustrates the ways in which elements of the R-I-T-E Model and the process of making Nav-Maps can be used both independently and with the assistance of a coach.

CAUGHT BETWEEN "SHOULD I STAY, OR SHOULD I GO?"

Vanessa was three years into a successful career at her professional services firm. She was noticed early and was promoted from a human resources coordinator to human resources business partner after just one year, which was somewhat rare. Believing that she would naturally continue her climb at the same pace

Table 7.1 Vanessa's Six-Question Matrix

1. _What Single Statement Best Describes Your Role?_ "I am a strategic and tactical HR business partner and my role is to help my division succeed."	
2. _What Tasks and Activities Absorb Most of Your Time?_ • Acting as an employee advocate • Implementing policies related to staffing, compensation, etc. • Managing resources and budgets • Planning and implementing individual and team professional development programs	**3. _What Are the Greatest Challenges that Prevent Your Best Work?_** • Responding to competing requests for resources and support • Managers seeking exceptions to policies to meet their unique circumstances • Getting people to buy-in to learning and development programs
4. _What Single Statement Reveals Your Vital Purpose to the Organization?_ "I make sure that the people-side of our operation is seamless so that our team can do its very best work. If I do not help solve problems, I'm in the way."	
5. _Which of Your Contributions Have the Greatest Value to the Organization?_ • Anticipating business needs and responding quickly with value-added solutions • Interpreting policy well, knowing when to balance compliance with flexibility • Adapting to fast-moving conditions and dealing with complex factors and changes that undermine our strategies • Communicating a clear, comprehensive picture of our needs to Corporate in order to effectively advocate for resources	**6. _What Are the Hidden Challenges of Delivering This Value?_** • Sorting through complaints to understand real issues that need immediate attention • Holding my ground under intense pressure from managers • Staying ahead of the change curve and figuring out how to spot issues before they blow up • Making time to communicate with Corporate • Not letting my own frustration about the pace of my career get in the way of my performance

and get promoted to a management position, two years later she was beginning to feel overlooked and underappreciated by her senior manager. The growing concern and resentment from feeling passed over left her caught between two equally strong questions: "Should I stay, or should I go?" After participating in a brief webinar that introduced the concepts and tools for going *beyond the job description* and achieving *breakthrough performance*, this is how Vanessa used the R-I-T-E Model to address her concerns in a self-guided process.

To begin, Vanessa focused on the "R"—Revealing the Hidden Curriculum of Work—and began to consider her vital purpose, value-added contributions, and hidden challenges. She completed the Six-Question Matrix in order to look within her everyday experience to catch a glimpse of her "job-within-the-job." Table 7.1 shows the final version of her Six-Question Matrix.

The experience of completing the Six-Question Matrix brought several important things to light for Vanessa. First, she realized a big irony; namely that in her job she tried to help other people identify their challenges to good work, but she had never done that for herself. As she scanned the final version of her matrix, she also realized that a typical day was usually set off-kilter with fires to put out and was not entirely consistent with her vital purpose. She also noticed that the subtle, but growing, frustration about the pace of her career was showing up in her attitude and starting to have an impact on the quality of her work. She wondered whether the combination of these two factors blocked some of her value-added contributions from being delivered.

After completing this exercise, next Vanessa took stock of what she learned thus far and documented some of the takeaways she gained from the process to this point, including:

- My job is definitely more complicated than I thought;
- I've been doing the easy things well, but I've avoided some of the tougher challenges;
- I'm starting to spot a few hidden barriers that cause stress for me and the team, and I will have to understand the root cause to get them resolved;
- When I get stuck, I tend to avoid telling anyone because I want to show that I can handle things on my own;
- I recognize that I have been off-purpose quite a bit in the last few months;
- I can see that some of my value-added contributions have been left on the sidelines;

- I acknowledge that I have been blaming others for some things, rather than taking full ownership for myself; and
- I wonder if my lack of promotion has more to do with my own performance, rather than being overlooked.

Now that Vanessa was starting to see a bigger picture, including the potential role she was playing in her own career frustration, she was interested in exploring this state of "feeling overwhelmed" by her priorities. She still could not shake the feeling that she *did not feel valued*, but she would return to that later. With momentum from her takeaways, she decided to make a Nav-Map to look more comprehensively at her concerns. She wrote her core barrier—I'm Overwhelmed by Priorities—at the center of her Nav-Map template in Figure 7.1.

DRAWING THE CONSTELLATION

The next step was to brainstorm the issues and obstacles that could potentially relate to the barrier of "being overwhelmed by priorities" in her work. On a scratch paper Vanessa listed possibilities by scanning her last several days and weeks on the job. She thought about the frustrations and concerns she experienced related to this core barrier and then began to narrow the list down. After brainstorming for a while, Vanessa turned back to the Nav-Map and completed the Constellation. Knowing that there is "no right answer" she kept an open

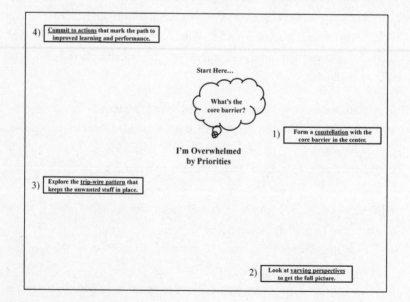

Figure 7.1 Starting the Nav-Map.

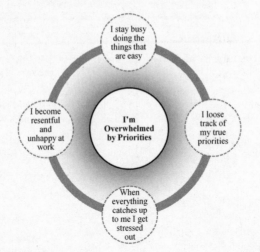

Figure 7.2   Vanessa's Constellation.

mind and filled in each peripheral circle with what she felt mattered. Her completed Constellation is illustrated in Figure 7.2.

Looking at her finished Constellation, Vanessa was struck by the way her core barrier of *getting overwhelmed* brought so many other challenges into play. She started to look at them as a system and realized that if she did not deal with the core concern, things would not be sustainable for her over time. This gave her a clearer picture of the paradox she felt on a daily basis: "I'm always busy, but never moving forward." By focusing on some of the easier tasks, but by avoiding the difficult challenges that require outside support, she was caught in the contradiction.

TESTING PERSPECTIVES

To continue the process, Vanessa moved to the VPB template in order to try to see things from her boss' perspective. As she wrestled with the competing impressions that she is both "overlooked" and responsible for "leaving her best contributions on the sideline," she thought it would help to play with various points of view. She knew that one option was to speak with her senior manager directly; however, for the first step she chose to project what he might say and see what she could learn. Figure 7.3 displays the contrasting VPBs that Vanessa documented.

As Vanessa compared the two viewpoints, she realized that her feelings of frustration were not really caused by the fact that she was overlooked. In fact, she reconsidered this conclusion and began to see that she was being challenged by

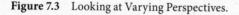

"Overlooked vs. Show Me More"

Vanessa	Senior Manager
• I work very hard, but my hard work is not noticed by my manager	• I know you're busy and that you work hard, but I wonder if you know what is most important
• I strive to show how independent/effective I can be	• I am available to support you, yet you don't seek out my input
• I believe my potential is being overlooked	• I believe in your potential, but I'm concerned about your level of stress

Figure 7.3   Looking at Varying Perspectives.

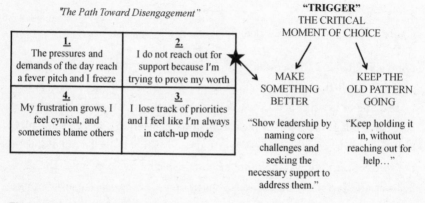

Figure 7.4   Vanessa's Trip-Wire Pattern.

her senior manager, but not necessarily being overlooked. As she read through her own bullet points, Vanessa connected a few more missing pieces in her way of thinking. She identified the difference between being "busy" and being "productive" and she realized that asking for support does not equal "incapable." While both of these insights were hard to sit with, she felt an emerging sense of *breakthrough* by just naming them.

SPOTTING THE TRIGGER

Next, Vanessa explored the underlying dynamic that potentially kept that feeling of frustration and blame in place. Although it was already fading a little bit, she knew it was a key to getting back on track. She completed the Trip-Wire Pattern template by filling in the four quadrants in sequence. She revisited her Constellation and the VPB template for ideas and put the final version together in Figure 7.4.

The work that she had already done made it easy for Vanessa to spot the trigger and name the choice/action that would make something different and shift the pattern. For her, it came down to confidently asking for help and support, rather than trying to go it alone. While she knew it might feel risky to potentially be seen as "incapable," she realized that she would just need to reframe it as "collaborating with a mentor."

THE ACTION PLAN

With growing confidence that she could transform her core barrier, Vanessa started the final step, which was to brainstorm about the concrete attitudes and behaviors that could move her away from the experience with the core barrier toward the aspirational learning and performance change she wanted in her professional life. Figure 7.5 illustrates Vanessa's final Action Continuum.

Once this final step was complete, she put each of the four parts together so that she had the completed Nav-Map on a single page. The finished version is reflected in Figure 7.6.

Following Vanessa's effort to reveal her hidden curriculum of work, she wrote a summary about her experience using the R-I-T-E Model and related tools for going Beyond the Job Description. She shared the following highlights:

"For me one of the biggest impacts was the chance to understand my job, including what I was doing to undermine my own performance. By looking in the mirror and coming to terms with what I brought to the table, I was able to focus more on my purpose and contributions, rather than on what somebody else was or was not doing for me. Seeing the hidden challenges that prevented my best work was also really important. It allowed me to make the Nav-Map, which I refer back

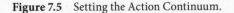

"When I Feel Valued, I Want to Grow"

Standing Still   **Learning & Growing**

The path from left to right.........

1. When I get overwhelmed – stop "keeping busy" and re-focus on what matters most

2. Ask for guidance when my true priorities are vague

3. Believe management understands and values my work

4. Remember that asking for support ≠ incapable

Figure 7.5   Setting the Action Continuum.

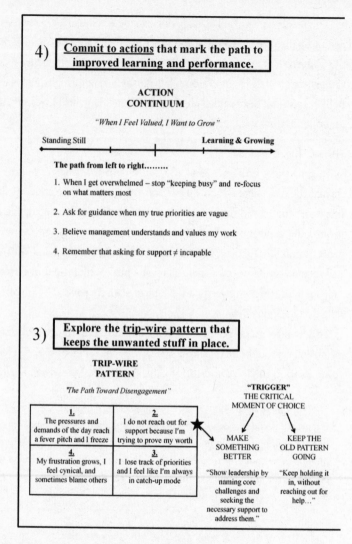

4) **Commit to actions** that mark the path to improved learning and performance.

**ACTION
CONTINUUM**

"When I Feel Valued, I Want to Grow"

Standing Still ←————————————|————————|————————→ **Learning & Growing**

The path from left to right.........

1. When I get overwhelmed – stop "keeping busy" and re-focus on what matters most

2. Ask for guidance when my true priorities are vague

3. Believe management understands and values my work

4. Remember that asking for support ≠ incapable

3) **Explore the trip-wire pattern that keeps the unwanted stuff in place.**

**TRIP-WIRE
PATTERN**

"The Path Toward Disengagement"

1. The pressures and demands of the day reach a fever pitch and I freeze	**2.** I do not reach out for support because I'm trying to prove my worth
4. My frustration grows, I feel cynical, and sometimes blame others	**3.** I lose track of priorities and I feel like I'm always in catch-up mode

"TRIGGER"
THE CRITICAL
MOMENT OF CHOICE

MAKE
SOMETHING
BETTER

KEEP THE
OLD PATTERN
GOING

"Show leadership by naming core challenges and seeking the necessary support to address them."

"Keep holding it in, without reaching out for help…"

Figure 7.6   Vanessa's Completed Nav-Map.

to on a weekly basis to make sure I'm on track with my actions. Since doing the first Nav-Map, I have made several additional Constellations and I'm working on Nav-Maps for other people to help them. The funny thing is that this was all right there; I just did not have a way to put it all together until now. I started out feeling like the most important question was 'Should I stay, or should I go?' but I quickly realized that it was the wrong question. For me, a better question is: 'Am I leading with my purpose, bringing my best contributions to the table, and taking ownership to resolve my hidden challenges at work?'"

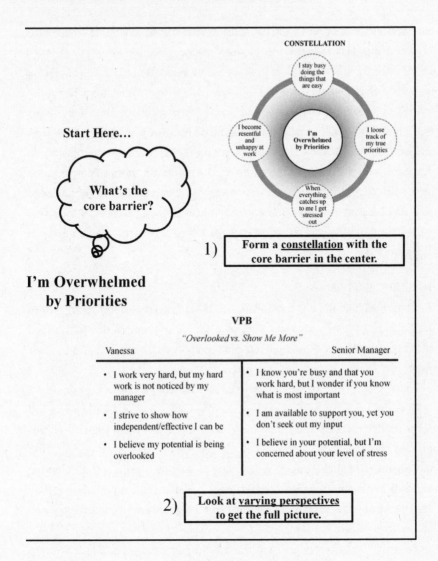

IN SEARCH OF BETTER COLLABORATION

Joel was a self-described "no-frills guy." At work he liked to get to the point without beating around the bush. He assessed his no-nonsense style of management as a good trait because it helped people address their issues quickly without getting embroiled in personality-driven concerns. With the same staff for a period of six years, Joel had been in a solid routine, the performance of his group was admired, and things worked well. However, after a series of changes and personnel turnover within his division, Joel started to wonder whether his standard approach to managing the team was still effective.

At a loss for what to do, Joel took the recommendation of his CEO and read an article that described the R-I-T-E Model and the related tools to resolve everyday leadership challenges. Curious, he began to experiment by drawing a few Constellations and ultimately made his own Nav-Map. This process helped him to assess his own perspective on the issues by drilling down into the core barrier that he observed most. During an impromptu conversation with Michael, one of his trusted team members, Joel realized that he needed to make a Nav-Map that reflected more than just his own perspective. As a first step, he invited Michael to collaborate on a Nav-Map. This is a summary of their process.

MAKING THE NAV-MAP

Because Joel had already completed a Nav-Map, it was important to him to let Michael lead with his ideas. Joel used the same prompts that had helped him earlier and he acted as both a facilitator and participant in their two-hour process:

Joel: "Thank you for your time today Michael; it's important to me that I understand what you and other team members are thinking. I know we've had some challenges lately and I want to get them right. A few days ago I used this process myself: it was quick and I found it helpful to clarify my thoughts about our organizational challenges. We're going to start by making a Constellation, which is just a picture of the interrelated issues that show up in our everyday experience at work. To start, let's brainstorm the question: *What challenges and concerns do you see in the team?*"

Michael: "I guess for me things have been going okay. I'm a little worried about our team meetings because they have not felt very productive. I appreciate that they are short because of how busy we are, but I also worry that some things are getting missed because of the lack of discussion."

Joel: "I have seen that too. You know how I like to run our meetings: short, to the point, and effective. I wonder if I have over-emphasized the 'short' part of things. What do you think the impact is of these abbreviated meetings?"

Michael: "Well, I think our collaboration isn't nearly what it used to be. People are acting independently trying to keep projects going, which is good in some ways, but not helpful in other ways. We're probably duplicating efforts quite a bit, which we can't afford to do. And, I think some of the new people on the team feel a bit rudderless."

Joel: "I think the irony is that by striving for so much efficiency, we are creating some unanticipated inefficiencies along the way. Okay, let's see if we can draw this out in the Constellation. For a placeholder in the center, let's just start with "Insufficient Communication Blocks Collaboration..."

Next, Joel and Michael worked together to complete the Constellation. In order to fill in the peripheral circles, they responded to the prompt: *"What else does this barrier create and what seems to be pushed and pulled into our everyday experience because of it?"* After a few back and forth exchanges, they made the Constellation in Figure 7.7.

Michael: "Wow, looking at this really simplifies the picture for me. I kind of see the cycle we've inadvertently made. Starting at the top of the circle, when we rush through our meetings, it really has a cascading effect on our ability to work together."

Joel: "I'm seeing it differently now too. What I thought was a strength is actually getting in the way of doing good work... This Constellation is just the first step; let's use the next phase to check into our different perspectives on the issue..."

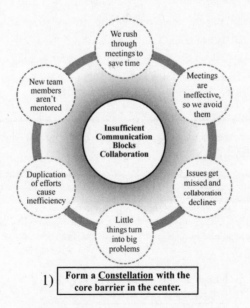

Figure 7.7   The Constellation of Insufficient Communication.

To continue, Joel introduced the concept of VPB. He wrote each of their names on one side of the T-Bar and then continued:

Joel: "Okay, this exercise should give us a chance to take a quick pause and gain a wider perspective on things before we jump into 'problem-solving mode.' The goal is to look at the issue honestly from different points of view; we're not trying to agree on how we look at the issue. Our task is to jot down a few bullet points that reflect the assumptions we have about the situation and the kinds of attitudes and behaviors that are in the mix. Here is a prompt to get started: *How do you see this issue playing out, and if you had to, what name would you give it?*"

Both Joel and Michael worked independently for a few minutes identifying and then refining their bullet points. When they were finished, they wrote them on the VPB template and discussed a possible title. Figure 7.8 shows their completed product.

As they scanned the finished product, Joel shared some discussion questions and he and Michael talked about them for a few minutes. The questions included: *What is similar and what is different about how we see things? What happens when we single out just one of the perspectives and call it "the right one" or the "truth?" And, now that there is a bigger picture here, in what ways might it be helpful to think about the varying perspectives?*

Michael: "Joel, thank you again for this opportunity to speak candidly. I hope that my perspective is not taken the wrong way."

"People Are Talking ... But Nobody Is Communicating"

Joel	Michael
• People can speak up when they want – my door is open	• I don't think it is a safe to raise concerns
• I assume that team members meet independently and collaborate as needed	• We need structured opportunities if we are going to talk about what matters
• We have a culture of trust because I don't micro-manage	• I don't trust that our leader knows what's happening because he is somewhat disconnected

2) **Look at <u>Varying Perspectives of Barriers</u> to get the full picture.**

Figure 7.8 Contrasting Both Perspectives.

Joel: "On the contrary, if you are feeling this way then others likely are too. I needed to hear that the pressure I put on everyone to stick with the way we've always done things is having an impact. I never would have thought that it was 'unsafe' for people to speak up, but I need to acknowledge that."

Michael: "When I look at your perspective, I want to thank you for the approach you take to let us do our jobs. The last thing I want is to be micro-managed or to experience 'death-by-meeting.' I think the assumption you have that we are independently talking and working together should be true, but it is just not the case."

Joel: "Okay, the fact that we are not looking at this as 'right vs. wrong' tells me that we are open-minded, which was the point of the last exercise. Let's go to the next stage and try to figure out if there is a flow to this pattern of communication and interaction. We are trying to spot the 'trigger point' where we could alter the conditions enough to disrupt the status quo..."

Using the Trip-Wire Pattern template as a guide, Joel and Michael started looking for the key actions that potentially created and sustained the situation. Using the four quadrants, they put each one in "sequence" going clockwise from top-left. They then identified where the critical moment of choice was (in this case it was box #3) and they put a star by it. Once they realized where the critical moment was, they looked at potential change by answering the question: *"What would we need to do differently to shift the pattern to something better?"* Figure 7.9 illustrates their Trip-Wire Pattern and the name that they gave it.

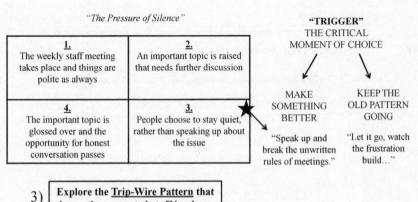

Figure 7.9   Spotting the Critical Moment in the Trip-Wire Pattern.

Michael: "I think we really hit on something. People are feeling frustrated, but collectively we are just going with the flow. The frustration is clearly building so it looks like we just need to speak up about it, even if that means starting a new expectation around our meetings."

Joel: "I agree; the way out of this mess is actually pretty straightforward. But, when you're on auto-pilot, you can't see it."

Michael: "I think we need to share this with the group."

Joel: "I agree; but before we do, there is one final step. This will help us identify some concrete actions to turn our 'frustrated silence' into a learning and performance goal that makes us a better team. We're going to plot the barrier on the left and the goal we've named on the right. Then we just need to be selective about 2–4 action steps that will move us from left to right toward the improvement we want to make. I really want the full team's input and buy-in on this, but let's get a draft started."

Figure 7.10 illustrates the working draft of their Action Continuum.

Joel: "Okay, now we're rolling; these are really good. I feel like we could bring these to the team, refine them, and then get buy-in. What do you think Michael?"

Michael: "I'm excited too. It is simple, but it addresses the root cause of the whole thing. The best part about this process was that it did not require any finger pointing or other confrontational discussions that could have made things worse. Let's roll it out to the team, get their input, and make it happen!"

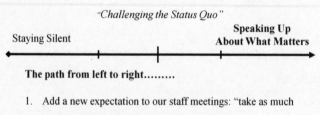

"Challenging the Status Quo"

Staying Silent   **Speaking Up About What Matters**

The path from left to right.........

1. Add a new expectation to our staff meetings: "take as much time as needed, but nothing more"
2. Know what's important, be willing to talk about it
3. Be hard on the problem, easy on the people
4. Remember: disagreement ≠ confrontation

4) **Commit to Actions** that mark the path to improved learning and performance.

Figure 7.10   A Game Plan for Talking about What Matters.

GOING FROM BLAME TO ACCOUNTABILITY IN THE TEAM

This final case study demonstrates the way members of a team can use the R-I-T-E Model to address their hidden challenges of work. It describes how the six-person executive management team of a large, international nonprofit organization navigated their tricky crossroads. Unlike the first two success stories, this process of achieving *breakthrough performance* was facilitated by an outside consultant who was familiar with the R-I-T-E Model. In order to provide useful detail to readers who may be in a position to facilitate this type of process for others, I have included some of the process cues and related steps.

AT THE CROSSROADS

Some of the organization's most successful programs (as measured by number of clients served, sustainable funding, and client satisfaction) were going to be discontinued in four months due to a combination of regulatory changes in their industry and financial limitations.[1] The team had recently held a series of strategy meetings that were intended to jumpstart a consensus-building process to reorient the organization around the changes and lay out an alternative five-year growth plan. After the first few meetings ended in acrimonious discussion, the CEO contacted a consultant to seek guidance in addressing what she called "our management team's surprising dysfunction."

The consultant met with the CEO in order to explore her goals for the consultation and to explain the R-I-T-E Model in more detail. The CEO was interested in having her team individually complete the Six-Question Matrix, but not until after they got some positive resolution on their pressing team challenge. After discussing the current situation, as well as various team members' perspectives on the presenting issues, the tentative design for the session focused on the middle two parts of the R-I-T-E Model.

IDENTIFYING BARRIERS

In most cases, the client's initial description of the problem acts as the "first draft" of the presenting issues. Veteran managers from the world of work understand the importance of treating these initial reactions as the first step toward venting frustrations and the start of slowly peeling back the layers to get to the core issue. To accelerate this process the consultant chose the BLPA, which he administered during the individual interviews conducted with each executive manager prior to the face-to-face meeting. After reviewing the individual assessments and assimilating those with the comments made during the interviews, the consultant created a snapshot of the most prominent learning and performance barriers affecting the team. These included:

1. **Tampering**—attempting to implement new behaviors and practices without changing the system that keeps old behaviors in place;
2. **Defensive Routines**—deflecting criticism, scapegoating, blaming other people or events, avoiding tasks, or behaving in ways that shift responsibility to others to prevent uncomfortable or embarrassing consequences;
3. **Getting Stuck in the Past**—clinging to a fixed, positive organizational identity from the past at the expense of current and accurate organizational assessments; and
4. **Performance Whitewashing**[2]—treating all goals and outcomes the same, thus diverting energy and attention from the most critical priorities.

DRAWING THE CONSTELLATION

At the first face-to-face meeting, the consultant began by sharing a summary of the interviews that reflected key themes and an inventory of the prominent issues identified. Using this as a starting place, the first step was to form a Constellation with the most frequently experienced barriers. The team took the initial list and reranked each core barrier on the same two-dimensional scale of frequency and impact that was in the BLPA. Based upon their rankings and subsequent discussion, *Defensive Routines* was the highest-ranked barrier. Once this barrier was selected as a starting place, they placed it in the core—at the center—of the Constellation in the template provided.

Next, a facilitated brainstorming session pinpointed several additional barriers that resulted from the presence/impact of the core barrier. As team members discussed peripheral barriers, they were encouraged not to worry about the wording, just to get ideas down in an objective way. Each individual wrote them in the outer circles in their Constellation worksheets while a group example was created on the whiteboard. If anyone got stuck, the consultant asked them to follow the question *"What else is this barrier creating?"* and that helped them to identify additional challenges. Figure 7.11 shows the completed Constellation.

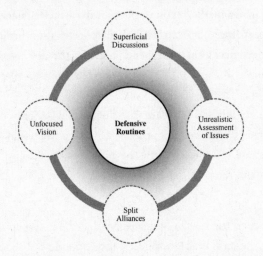

Figure 7.11   Completed Constellation.

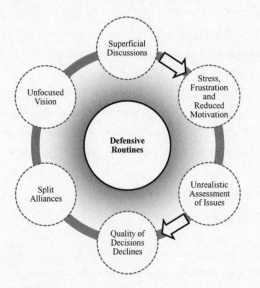

Figure 7.12   The Extended Constellation.

The process of noticing and developing a deeper awareness of barriers is a critical moment in the R-I-T-E Model, so once the team developed the Constellation and affirmed that it was consistent with their shared experience in recent manager's meetings, the consultant asked them to take it all in for a reflective moment. During discussion about the Constellation, the consultant invited the team to further explore the nature of the barriers, including an assessment regarding other effects that the constellation brought into their individual experience. One team member shared the example of an expanding Constellation in Figure 7.12, which reveals the personal impact from barriers.

The consultant advised the team that they would later return to the other prominent barriers and repeat the process of forming additional Constellations. However, continuing to work with the most widely acknowledged barrier required a move to the next step in the process.

VPB

In order to deepen the sense of perspective that the group could take on the Constellation, the consultant introduced the concept of VPB. Several people had used the phrase "pushing back," and the consultant drew a grid and put "Forms of Resistance" at the top. Labeling one perspective "pushing back for the wrong reasons" and the other one "pushing back for the right reasons," the consultant invited the group to play with the various perspectives that they have taken themselves or seen others take according to the labels. Figure 7.13 provides a picture of what they documented.

The exercise used to create the VPB snapshot resulted in a lively discussion about the last few difficult meetings. One member of the group offered a very candid summary of the VPB when he said: *"It looks like there is a pretty fine line between naming the problem with the rationale to stop moving forward and naming the problem with the requirements to move forward. Personally I would like to be on the right-end of that VPB."*

	"Forms of Resistance"	
Pushing Back for the Wrong Reasons	Pushing Back for the Right Reasons
• This is really hard and overwhelming and we can't do it alone	• This is really difficult and overwhelming, which means we may need additional support
• We have too many other priorities to get to so we can set this aside	• We have other priorities, but this is at the top so we we'll set lesser priorities aside first
• It is too complex to understand so we will have to wait until it gets clearer	• This is complex, so all the more reason to be decisive with the "unknowns"

Figure 7.13   VPB—Forms of Resistance.

With these clarifying statements as a transitional moment, the consultant moved the group to the next phase in the sequence.

SPOTTING THE TRIP-WIRE PATTERN

Next, the consultant introduced the concept of Trip-Wire Patterns and explained what is required to truly transform barriers. Trip-Wire Patterns help you visually depict the causes and conditions that keep barriers in place and spot the critical intervention that could alter those conditions enough to disrupt the status quo and make it feasible for new circumstances to emerge. To help the management team identify and shift their Trip-Wire Pattern, a four-quadrant template was presented. Utilizing his full range of observations from the session, as well as the disclosures made during the initial interviews, the consultant began to plot out the basic pattern that sustained the core barrier. The process included a lot of reality testing with the team. When something was written, the consultant would test for accuracy before moving to the next quadrant.

Once the four parts of the pattern were confirmed, the consultant asked: *"Where is the trigger point that activates this Trip-Wire Pattern and keeps the team stuck?"* To produce open-minded responses to the prompt, the consultant restated the natural progression of the pattern to help them to see how the sequence typically unfolded. In this way, the "shoulds" and "knee-jerk reactions" were discussed. Even though everyone recognized that the pattern did not create desirable outcomes, they could see the attitudes/assumptions that kept it in place. Figure 7.14 illustrates this clockwise process and the goal of identifying the pattern's "trigger" indicated by a star.

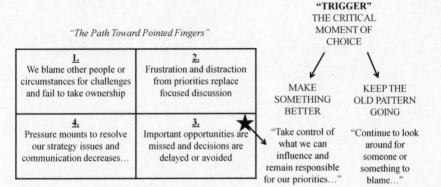

Figure 7.14   Trip-Wire Pattern with Identified Trigger.

With the trigger identified, the consultant invited the group to discuss and agree to a response if/when the trigger resurfaces. This led to the final step in the process, setting the Action Continuum.

SETTING THE ACTION CONTINUUM

To help the team establish their action plan for moving forward, the consultant returned to the core barrier from the completed Constellation. The core barrier was plotted on the left side of the Action Continuum and its inverse learning and performance aspiration was plotted to the right. To identify the element of learning and performance, the consultant invited open discussion using the following prompt: *"What attitudes, beliefs, or actions would be required to overcome this core barrier?"* As individuals responded to the question, the consultant graphically documented ideas and underscored similar responses. Absolute consensus was not required, so the consultant simply asked clarifying questions along the way to test the relevance and discern the most commonly held descriptions.

Participants were encouraged to refine their language from abstract to concrete and committed. As the discussion progressed, the consultant purposely framed the exercise in terms of identifying 2–4 actions steps in order to concentrate the group around a smaller number of achievable steps. The team ultimately agreed upon the following three action steps, which are documented in Figure 7.15.

As the final session transitioned to closure and next steps, the consultant offered his perspective on culture change and ways to get the most return on the positive benefits of the consultation. He then invited the management team

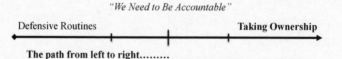

"We Need to Be Accountable"

Defensive Routines   **Taking Ownership**

The path from left to right.........

1. Document our shared expectations for communication

2. If a defensive routine surfaces: name it (but don't blame it)

3. Commit to longer meetings with ample discussion time

4. If decisions are sidetracked and frustration sets in, take a break and get back on track

Figure 7.15   Action Steps for Improved Team Learning and Performance.

to reflect on ways to use their experience in the meeting as a catalyst for deeper organizational change. Within their own team, they committed to sticking with the process as the need to revisit old issues and address new ones emerged. For those who managed larger divisions, there was a commitment to utilize the R-I-T-E Model to help their own teams apply a constructive approach to dealing with a variety of organizational issues.

KEY TAKEAWAYS

The R-I-T-E Model is a compass to guide you in the fast-changing world of work. Rather than a prescriptive process, it is an array of signposts that support the implementation of the concepts and tools required to go *beyond the job description* and achieve *breakthrough performance*. Case studies from the real world of work demonstrate how the sequence acts as a loose guide to follow, either in a self-directed manner, or with the assistance of a manager, coach, or consultant.

As a powerful tool for personal and professional development, the R-I-T-E Model can be used to see the hidden side of work and get individuals on a path toward success in their own careers. From a team standpoint, the R-I-T-E Model can also be used in a variety of situations, including:

- Identifying and resolving individual challenges at work;
- Evaluating the general status of a working relationship;
- Reviewing a specific episode of communication and interaction with a colleague that produced an unwanted outcome or experience;
- Identifying patterns that may need to be altered in order to successfully implement a specific change in the team or organization; and
- Exploring potential causes of unwanted or unexpected changes (e.g., decreased engagement among employees, silence where there was active communication, etc.).

Chapter 8

MAKING YOUR OWN NAV-MAPS

WHEN YOU BREAK IT DOWN to the simplest level, there are only four questions you must answer to transform your hidden challenges at work into opportunities for improved learning and performance: (1) What is the root cause of my challenge? (2) How can I see it from various perspectives to get the full picture? (3) What underlying pattern holds the unwanted experience and outcomes in place? (4) And, what action can I take to resolve the challenge?

Nav-Maps are the preferred way of working through the four questions; however, if drawing Constellations and the other models ever feels too complicated, I suggest using *the simplest combination of tools and approaches* that can be used to *most effectively create the change you want to see.* This means that rather than trying to "do the process right" you simply do what is useful, no matter how far off script you need to go.

Using these progressive questions as a guide, you can turn everyday obstacles at work into pathways for better performance and increased quality of working life. Making Nav-Maps is something that anyone can do with a little practice. This chapter builds on the information provided in the last two and provides a guide for you to start making your own Nav-Maps. It begins with identifying the core barrier and continues through each of the four progressive steps. As you begin to make your own Nav-Maps, here is a quick recap of each individual stage.

DETERMINE THE CORE BARRIER

Take a look at this short list of common barriers from the BLPA. Is one of these the likely source of your headache?

- Absence of dialogue and limited expression of diverse viewpoints
- Accomplishing lesser priorities well while failing to focus on more important objectives
- Lack of reflection and learning from past successes and failures
- An organizational culture in which individuals experience fear and distrust
- Inability or unwillingness to adapt to fast-changing, complex, or uncertain conditions
- Anxiety, distraction, or avoidance due to communication and information overload
- Attempting to implement new behaviors and practices without changing the system that keeps old behaviors in place
- Attributing successes to one's own abilities and efforts while blaming failures on other people or circumstances

If not, write what you think the core barrier is (5 words or less).

Besides yourself, who is the one other person most affected by this and what is their relationship (e.g., co-worker, boss, etc.)?

How do you think the other person would describe the issue (10 words or less)?

On a scale of 1–5, where "5" is extremely urgent and "1" is not urgent at all, how important is it to you to get this headache resolved?

STEP ONE: FORM A CONSTELLATION WITH THE CORE BARRIER IN THE CENTER

A Constellation is an image that connects all of the related issues together. Constellations are helpful because they allow us to sort through the peripheral junk to find the core issues that really need our attention. They can make us realize why the situation is causing such a headache—there is a lot of interconnected *stuff* going on! Using Figure 8.1, create your own Constellation with the core barrier at the center and its related peripheral barriers along the edges.

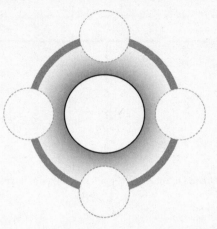

Figure 8.1   Template to Create a Constellation of Barriers.

STEP TWO: LOOK AT VARIOUS PERSPECTIVES TO GET THE FULL PICTURE

Identifying and comparing different perspectives creates a clearer picture of what is going on. In this way you can step back from quick conclusions and see how people with similar intentions can end up with such different points of view. The best part about this is the recognition that so often we just "assume we know what others are thinking" when we really don't have the full picture. Using Figure 8.2, discover the VPB to see the full picture.

STEP THREE: EXPLORE TRIP-WIRE PATTERNS THAT KEEP THE UNWANTED OUTCOMES IN PLACE

Once broader viewpoints are exchanged, Trip-Wire Patterns illustrate how the unwanted experiences are often held in place out of the force of habit. They can also reveal the critical moment where something needs to change if the pattern caused by the core barrier is going to "shift to something better," or remain in the same unhealthy routine. Using Figure 8.3, map the quadrants that reflect the underlying pattern that keeps the behavior and experience in place.

STEP FOUR: COMMIT TO ACTIONS THAT MARK THE PATH TO IMPROVED LEARNING AND PERFORMANCE

The final step includes a short set of goals that, if implemented, can lead to the desired change. This is the time to identify and commit to a few key actions that

Figure 8.2   Template to Discover Varying Perspectives of Barriers.

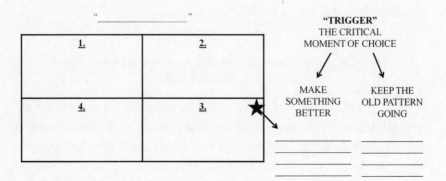

Figure 8.3   Template to Map the Trip Wire Pattern.

will transform the headache into a useful insight that boosts learning and performance and gets your working life back on track. You do not need 27 new things to do, but having 2–4 really focused action steps can begin the process of moving from left (the barrier) to right (the desired change). Using Figure 8.4, plot the action steps that are required to move from left to right along the continuum.

After reviewing each of the four steps, you can see that individually each one holds some value, but taken together, the completed Nav-Map provides a framework for transforming barriers. If you want to put them all together you can transfer them to the blank Nav-Map template in Figure 8.5. Moving forward, the completed Nav-Map is your reference to moving past the challenges you face in the world of work.

With these process steps as a guide you can generate your own Nav-Maps to resolve barriers and take control of your path to success at work. Over time you

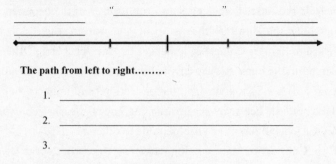

The path from left to right.........

1. _____

2. _____

3. _____

Figure 8.4   Template to Plot the Action Continuum.

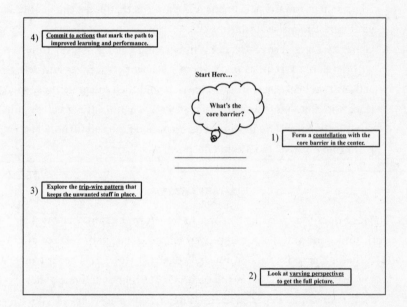

Figure 8.5   Nav-Map Template.

will notice that there are ancillary benefits that surface with the process. Not only do barriers get addressed in effective ways, but you gain developmental skills that extend your capacity to successfully make Nav-Maps. These include the ability to:

1. See Subtle Challenges That Blindside Others—You will develop the visual capacity to notice the barriers to learning and performance that are all around you. You can then draw your world of work in a way that

reveals the hidden challenges and root causes of the experiences and outcomes that diminish the quality of your working life.

2. Learn to Express Complex Challenges In Ways That Help Others—You can build the linguistic capacity to express the causes and conditions of your barriers, as well as the interconnections and impacts they create. This not only helps you process the ongoing challenges you experience on the job, but serves as a useful guide to others.

3. Gain Confidence Manipulating Barriers—You learn to practice mental flexibility and use problem-solving dexterity to change the root-cause factors that fuel and sustain barriers. Rather than being stuck in patterns of behavior that hinder your performance, you will spot ways to trigger them toward new habits and patterns that boost the quality of your performance and working life.

4. Generate Long-Term Success by Integrating Change—Over time you will develop a system to make room for new perspectives and related actions that help you transform barriers and then integrate those solutions back into your working life, as well as within the greater team/ organizational system in which you operate. These will turn short-term gains into positive, long-term effects.

KEY TAKEAWAYS

The four questions you must answer to transform hidden challenges at work into opportunities for improved learning and performance are: (1) What is the root cause of my challenge? (2) How can I see it from various perspectives to get the full picture? (3) What underlying pattern holds the unwanted experience and outcomes in place? and (4) What action can I take to resolve the challenge? Nav-Maps are the preferred way of working through these four questions to discover the pathway for better performance and increased quality of working life. Making a Nav-Map begins with identifying the core barrier and continues through each of the four progressive steps – creating the Constellation, charting the VPB, identifying the Trip-Wire Pattern, and plotting the Action Continuum.

Chapter 9

QUANTIFY YOUR INVESTMENT

THE FACT THAT YOU ARE still reading this book likely means that you believe the investment of your time and energy required to implement the book's concepts will pay off. Despite this potential upside, you may still be wresting with the question *"How will I find the time to make it happen?"* For many people, their first answer could be *"This sounds nice, but in reality I don't have the time or energy to slow down, make Nav-Maps, and think about the hidden side of work."* The reality is that you already spend considerable time responding to your hidden curriculum of work. You just do it without a flashlight and map.

If you are serious about getting on purpose and leading with your greatest contributions, the question is not "Where will you find the time?" The better question is: "How can you afford not to make the time necessary to implement these changes?"

The purpose of this brief chapter is to establish a logic model that demonstrates just how much time you have at your disposal, including specific ways in which you can leverage your existing work load to accelerate your implementation of *Beyond the Job Description*. With some common sense and a little bit of math I will show you how to convert a minimum of 28 percent of your time and effort at work into an investment in your own working life.

To begin, let's assume you work full time, which is the equivalent of 2080 hours per year (40 hours per week x 52 weeks = 2080). How do you spend the majority of your time? One of the best ways to generalize about what people do on the job is to look at the one cross-cutting feature that we share in our working lives. Regardless of the role we play within the industry we work, we attend lots of **meetings**.

On a really bad day, a cynical view of meetings could include this definition: "A meeting is an interaction where the unwilling, selected from the uninformed, led by the unsuitable, to discuss the unnecessary, are required to write a report about the unimportant."[1] On a good day, we may look at meetings as the chance to *connect with people, discuss important matters, and align resources, priorities, and actions to get great work done.* The reality for most of us is that the quality of our meetings falls somewhere in the middle of these two extremes.

Whatever we call them—stand-up meetings, sit-down discussions, team gatherings, all-hands town hall meetings, 1:1 conversations, etc.—nobody can escape participation in at least a few of them. The paradox of meetings is that they "dominate workers' and managers' time and yet are considered to be costly, unproductive, and dissatisfying."[2]

The frequency and duration of meetings is actually on the rise, and managers and workers already spend anywhere between 25 and 80 percent of their time in meetings. For a full-time worker, this translates to time in meetings from 520 hours (or 65 full working days) to 1,664 hours (or 208 full working days). Does your rear end hurt just thinking about all that sitting?

The point of all of this is that the presenting side of work—the SMW—shows up at the intersection of all these meetings. If you use your existing load of meetings to begin exploring your hidden curriculum of work, you leverage the time you would already spend for a higher-value pursuit.

Using these statistics as baseline data, you can compare the cost/benefit analysis of investing time and energy in your path to success at work. Even if you spend only 25 percent of your time at meetings (the low end of the range), that amounts to 65 full working days per year where you presumably talk about getting work done or talk about why work didn't get done. If you are going to spend 25 percent of your time in meetings, it is safe to say that, to some extent, *meetings are your job.* Because the quality and value of meetings varies, it is also safe to say that there will be some "wasted days" along the way. Knowing this, how much time do you believe is worth *investing in yourself* to focus o the quality of your working life and the performance outcomes you achieve?

Let's say you believe that out of the 100 percent of your total time on the job, it is worth it to you to spend 3 percent of your time focusing on meeting the true challenges of your work and succeeding in your career. (I think you are worth more time, but let's go with 3 percent for now.) This is the equivalent of 62.4 hours or about eight full working days per year. This breaks down to 5.3 hours per month, 1.3 hours per week, and 15 minutes per day. *Fifteen minutes per day;* even this small, incremental contribution can make a significant difference. A few minutes in the morning, to focus on your priorities and check-in on the challenges and opportunities before you, then a few minutes at the end of the day, to reflect on what happened and what you can learn and integrate for tomorrow, can make a significant impact on your ability to see the hidden side of work.

In order to turn your 3 percent into 28 percent (i.e. 3 percent of your basic investment into your on-going learning and performance plus 25 percent of your existing time spent at meetings), simply piggy back on your existing meeting schedule with a parallel process of navigating the hidden curriculum of work. This is no more than a little common sense and math. On your walk to the meeting room, while you are seated waiting for others to arrive, or at your work station before you join the conference call, imagine if you took a couple of minutes prior to every meeting to think through three questions that are inspired by the Six-Question Matrix and your "job-within-the-job:"

1. What vital purpose can I play at this meeting?
2. What contributions can I deliver during this meeting that will add the greatest value?
3. What potential challenges could surface and make it hard for me/us to have a successful meeting and achieve the results we need?

Working through these questions not only provides a way to improve the quality of your experience and outcomes at meetings, but it is also a way for you to systemically expose your "job-within-the-job" at the places it commonly shows up. You will thank yourself for the investment and others will notice too. Once you get in the habit of using your meetings to explore your hidden challenges at work, you can use time outside of meetings to take on additional endeavors that bring your vital purpose and value-added contributions to the forefront.

KEY TAKEAWAYS

The availability of *time* and *energy* is one of the biggest variables in any personal and professional development effort. Even when we can see the potential upside of a change, we must still confront the question: *Where will I find the time to make it happen?* Going *beyond the job description* and achieving *breakthrough performance* is within reach for everyone, and the availability of discretionary time and energy required to discover your hidden path to success expands exponentially when you apply a basic logic model.

Analyzing a time study of your existing work load, including the meeting schedule that you already keep, demonstrates just how much time you likely have at your disposal. Using three questions inspired by your "job-within-the-job"—*What vital purpose can I play at this meeting? What contributions can I deliver during this meeting that will add the greatest value? What potential challenges could surface and make it hard for me/us to have a successful meeting and achieve the results we need to?*—you can leverage your existing workload to accelerate your implementation of *Beyond the Job Description.*

Chapter 10

THE ANSWER TO OVERWORKED AND DISENGAGED

CHAPTER 1 DESCRIBED THE COSTS OF chronic disengagement at work. The epidemic wreaks havoc on the quality of our working lives while simultaneously causing a steep decline in the quality and impact of work that can be measured against organizational bottom lines in the billions. Approximately "seventy-one percent of American workers are 'not engaged' or 'actively disengaged' in their work, meaning they are emotionally disconnected from their workplaces and are less likely to be productive."[1] Specific estimates about the percentage of actively disengaged workers vary, but it is likely as high as 26 percent.[2] And the Gallup organization estimates that total employee disengagement costs the US economy as much as $350 billion annually![3]

Now I want to go beyond the statistics and make this personal. I do not need fancy words to break this down, nor do I need an elaborate assessment to tell you what you already know: *it is an ongoing struggle to stay engaged at work*. The true challenges of the hidden side of work erode the quality of our working lives and zap our motivation to stay present and invest fully in what we are doing. Because the hidden curriculum of work keeps many of our everyday challenges just out of plain sight, the anxiety and stress they cause is ever-present, but never fully addressed. While this book is a lifeline for that troubled 26 percent of workers, it is also a vital tool for the rest of us who are not actively disengaged, but who nonetheless struggle to meet the demands of our hidden curriculum of work.

You may not have mentally "quit your job" and you may not experience the full brunt of chronic disengagement, however, when it comes right down to it: *if you are just not that engaged in your work then you put the quality of your working life and the trajectory of your career at risk.*

Most of us juggle work and personal life along with a variety of family, social, and community commitments. We are responsible for greater productivity with fewer resources, which leaves us feeling overworked and exhausted. Worries about the future are always in the back of our minds because organizations no longer provide predictable job security or sponsor ongoing career and professional development. And, in this environment of constant change where there is little margin for anything "extra," even basic challenges can put us over the edge and undermine our best work.

As far as I know, there is no alternative world where every day is a great day on the job, where people are always fully present and excited about what they do, where people remain in sync with their values and priorities at all times, and where the challenges people encounter simply bounce off with little effect. In the real world of work it is a struggle to *work well.* We get knocked down. We receive bad news. Our priorities and goals become clouded. Our values get tested. And the challenges we face can punch us right in the gut. While this stark picture reflects the incline of our working lives, it does not mean that meeting its demands with focus and confidence cannot be done.

During my graduate studies I was fortunate to work with one of the luminaries from the field of organization development, the late Charlie Seashore. As a member of my dissertation committee, Charlie gave me important advice at a key turning point in my education. During an early committee meeting where my topic—a study that would explore the hidden challenges of learning and performance at work—was just beginning to emerge, I proceeded to pontificate about how grand the study would be and just how academic (read confusing) I could make it. In an equally supportive/challenging voice that only a mentor could deliver, Charlie pushed my pages aside, looked me in the eye, and said: "We want to see Jesse in this study. The world needs to see Jesse." In the same way, the world needs to see more of you, too. A working life that is consistent with what matters to you will bring your best to the forefront. When your capacity to work well hangs in the balance somewhere between the "struggle to engage" and the desire to "check out," your best efforts are always limited.

The answer to overworked and disengaged starts with *bringing **you** to the fore-front* and *taking back your influence* over work. In the big picture, you need to *establish a vision for your working life* that inspires you to do your best work.

You need a plan that will help you stand out, stay ahead of the change curve, and push you to contribute more of *you*. With an eye toward the everyday, you need to stop interpreting your work through your standard job description and quit waiting for opportunities to show people what you can do. When you operate in the SMW, you take a back seat in your own working life. If you will not step forward to drive, who will? If you are not willing to do that right now, when will it happen?

To regain your power you have to create your own path to success at work by looking within your job description to discover your "job-within-the-job." By clarifying your vital purpose and value-added contributions, and then coming face-to-face with your hidden challenges, you will work well over time and add increasing value to the organization. When you find that *mutual agenda* that aligns your contributions and needs with the needs of your team and organization, you will stand out, stay relevant, and thrive in your world of work.

Here is how the physics of this change can happen. The state of being *over-worked and disengaged* is a presenting condition. The root causes include things like confusing roles and responsibilities, meaningless tasks and activities that do not inspire or challenge you, difficult people and circumstances that create ongoing confusion and stress, lack of clarity and focus about your vital purpose and value-added contributions, and the many unresolved challenges that prevent you from doing your best work.

The impact of this condition on your experience at work can include many of the chronic disengagement effects already described, including withdrawal behaviors (e.g., tardiness, missing deadlines, and slowly checking out); cycles of burnout (e.g., insufficient sleep, stress from too many unmet responsibilities, fatigue, and disconnection from the values and aspirations that can reenergize you); and performance declines (e.g., decreases in the quality and accuracy of your work, failure to follow through on critical priorities, and the loss of trust and credibility with others).

In order to shift the presenting conditions so that something new can emerge, you have to first change the underlying patterns of thought and behavior that keep the conditions of "overworked and disengaged" in place. The interesting thing here is that, rather than beginning solely with a change in thought to achieve the new state of mind, I want you to start with a change of behavior as well.

I have provided tools for you to look at the hidden side of work and to see things for what they are. I have given you a framework to do the heavy lifting to discover your "job-within-the-job" and then stay on your hidden path to success by transforming your everyday challenges with Nav-Maps. If you take action on these things, then you will enjoy many positive changes that follow. It is all up to you. The new state of being, or presenting conditions from this shift in thinking and action, will take you from "overworked and disengaged" to *energized, engaged,* and *on course to achieve the working life you want.*

DO YOU KNOW WHAT YOU WANT?

There is a basic assumption in all of this that relates to your capacity to defini-tively say *what it is you want* and *why it matters.* To conclude this chapter here is a deeper treatment of this important issue.

The answer to overworked and disengaged begins with active steps to remake your working life. Where the rubber meets the road, the critical element of this is to *know what you want.* If you could remake the day-to-day experience you have at work into something better, what would you make?

Uncovering your hidden path to success at work requires the capacity to talk about what matters. This is not a psychology book, nor do I have any desire to summarize the complex reasons why some of us suppress our willingness to advocate for our interests at certain times. However, there are four common issues that, if addressed, can be turned into opportunities for better communi-cation about your values and priorities.[4]

The first issue is that *we are often very good at wanting what others want, but unpracticed at wanting stuff that is consistent with who we are and what we value.* The interesting aspect of this is that we are continuously in the act of striving toward something—even when it feels as though we are not. In his 2009 TED talk,[5] the internationally acclaimed writer, philosopher, and com-mentator on work, Alain de Botton, described the challenge of distinguishing what matters to us and the noise we hear from the world:

> One of the interesting things about success is that we think we know what it means. A lot of the time our ideas about what it would mean to live successfully

are not our own. They're sucked in from other people... [It] is not that we should give up on our ideas of success, but that we should make sure that they are our own. We should...make sure that we own them, that we're truly the authors of our own ambitions. Because it's bad enough not getting what you want, but it's even worse to have an idea of what it is you want and find out at the end of the journey that it isn't, in fact, what you wanted all along.

The second issue is that in the absence of clearly stating what matters, *you will make people guess and they will likely guess incorrectly*. Most conflict in the workplace occurs due to unmet needs. The irony of unmet needs and expectations is that they are often left unspoken. So when we rationalize ourselves away from clearly stating what we want, or what is most important to us in a specific situation or relationship, we may think that we are avoiding the pitfall. The fact is we are simply digging the hole deeper by forcing the other person or people to guess our relative perspective and priorities and to take action accordingly.

The third issue is that *getting what you want requires active movement toward it*. It is self-deception to want something, but to make no active move toward it. The first move is usually naming what that thing is—no matter how vague it may seem at the moment. Gaining the confidence to talk out loud about what matters is an active move.

The fourth issue is that pursuing our vital purpose and value-added contributions requires us to *say yes* and *no in the right ways, at the right times*. In other words, we need equal amounts of courage and willingness to start doing the things that, despite their potential difficulty, are required to make something different. We also need the courage and willingness to say no, draw a line in the sand, and avoid doing certain other things that would either reestablish the SMW or simply get in the way of making what we want.

Saying "yes" to new things is more straightforward than saying "no." We know that there are truly no individual actors in organizations and, regardless of your title, tenure, and power in the organization, you need other people. But when the writer and cartoonist Hugh MacLeod said that "the best way to get approval is not to need it," he points to a very important theme with regard to taking the wheel in our working lives.

When there is something we want, we have to be willing to talk about it in the language of our priorities (but in a way that reflects the mutual agenda where our individual needs and aspirations intersect with team and organizational priorities). If we are willing to share our own vision of what matters and work openly with others, we naturally move beyond the need for "approval" to active "engagement" and support for our own goals.

THE COST OF UNMITIGATED BARRIERS

In the next chapter you will have the opportunity to create a Future-Proof Plan. Prior to establishing your plan, one useful way of taking stock of your motivation to get Future-Proofed is to assess the costs of unmitigated barriers in your working life. When left unresolved for too long, these everyday challenges make your plate feel like it is overflowing as they destroy your energy, motivation, and desire to engage.

In order to measure these adverse impacts you can use the Impact Map in Figure 10.1 as a prompt. In each of the four quadrants, assess what impact your most challenging barriers have on the quality of your work, working relationships, personal health and well-being, and personal life. The goal of completing this Impact Map is to honestly assess the effects of barriers and to assess what is at stake here if you leave them unresolved.

As you scan your completed Impact Map, what do you see? Does coming face-to-face with the real costs of your unresolved barriers give you more incentive to develop a Future-Proof Plan that will help you stand out and stay ahead of the change curve?

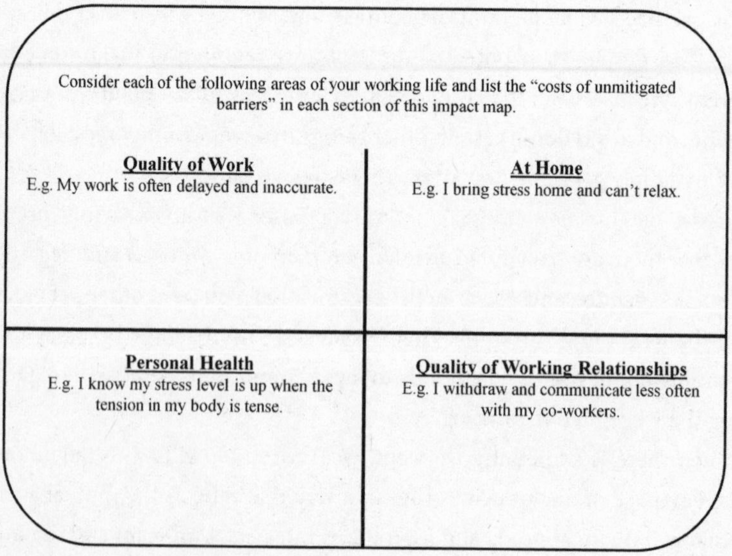

Consider each of the following areas of your working life and list the "costs of unmitigated barriers" in each section of this impact map.

Quality of Work	**At Home**
E.g. My work is often delayed and inaccurate.	E.g. I bring stress home and can't relax.
Personal Health	**Quality of Working Relationships**
E.g. I know my stress level is up when the tension in my body is tense.	E.g. I withdraw and communicate less often with my co-workers.

Figure 10.1   Impact Map of Unmitigated Barriers.

KEY TAKEAWAYS

Chronic disengagement at work is an epidemic that wreaks havoc on the quality of our working lives while simultaneously causing a steep decline in the quality and impact of work that can be measured against organizational bottom lines in the billions. The percentage of actively disengaged workers is likely as high as 26 percent and the Gallup organization estimates that total employee disengagement costs the US economy as much as $350 billion annually. The answer to overworked and disengaged starts with *bringing* **you** *to the forefront* and *taking back your influence* over work.

In the big picture, this personal revolution starts by *establishing a vision for your working life* that inspires you to do your best work. You need a plan that will help you stand out, stay ahead of the change curve, and push you to contribute more of *you*. With an eye toward the everyday, you need to stop interpreting your work through your standard job description and quit waiting for opportunities to show people what you can do.

To regain your power you have to create your own path to success at work by clarifying your vital purpose and value-added contributions and then coming face-to-face with your hidden challenges. When you find that *mutual agenda* that aligns your contributions and needs with the needs of your team and organization, you will stand out, stay relevant, and thrive in your world of work. All of this requires that you *know what you want*.

The issues that you will likely face as you set out to discover your hidden path to success at work include finding your voice and a language for expressing your vision for a better way to work, communicating this clearly with the critical working relationships that can support you, and actively moving toward that vision through adversity. If you are still unsure about the value of making a Future-Proof Plan, completing the Impact Map that reveals the costs of your unresolved barriers will convince you about the value.

Chapter 11

CREATE YOUR
FUTURE-PROOF PLAN

YOU ARE CONVINCED THAT YOU want to take the driver's seat in your working life and do what is necessary to stand out, stay ahead of the change curve, and get Future-Proofed. The purpose of this chapter is to help you create your individual Future-Proof Plan that will successfully lead you through this process.

Previous chapters in this book showed you how to identify and resolve the hidden challenges that make it hard for you to get your best work done. Now the focus shifts toward refining and integrating your vital purpose and value-added contributions with a substantive vision for your working life. The three steps to create your customized Future-Proof Plan are to:

1. *Take the Self-Assessment—"How Future-Proof Are You?"*
2. *Visualize Your Horizon—Create Goals for Your Working Life*
3. *Map the Strategy—Plot a Course for the Working Life You Want*
   - Refine Your Future-Proof Purpose
   - Clarify Your Future-Proof Contributions
   - Identify Your Future-Proof Capabilities
   - Establish Your Future-Proof Relationships

Prior to describing these three steps in detail, a more precise definition of a Future-Proof Plan is needed, including an explanation of the value it holds for you and the required flexibility you must build into your plan.

WHAT IS A FUTURE-PROOF PLAN?

A *Future-Proof Plan* is the sequence of critical milestones that represent a realistic path toward achieving your long-term career goals. Rather than traditional career development approaches from the SMW (think resume-writing, etc.) this approach is inspired by the hidden curriculum of work. Guided by the principles and practices that can help you stand out, stay ahead of the change curve, and achieve the working life you want, your Future-Proof plan is like a tightly packed synopsis of your vision and strategy for success on the job.

With insights that reflect the work you have already done to implement the concepts and practices of *Beyond the Job Description,* your plan will be customized with additional exercises suggested throughout this chapter. Above everything else, your Future-Proof Plan is based on *your own* wisdom, intelligence, and discipline—not on anybody else's expectations of you or their prescriptions for what you should do.

> **Wisdom** is seeing the hidden side of work in the everyday experiences you have on the job. **Intelligence** is discovering the mutual agenda that aligns your purpose, contributions, and career aspirations with the needs of the team and greater organization. **Discipline** is navigating the true demands of your work and leveraging your vital purpose and value-added contributions in an ongoing effort to resolve barriers, get *beyond the job description*, and stay on your path to *breakthrough performance.*

The reality for most of us is that work never stands still. We change jobs, move on to new companies, and cross over into different careers. Considering this movement, the teams and organizations we join will require a different mix of knowledge, skills, abilities, and overall contributions from us. Although we all operate from a core set of strengths and capabilities, *our vital purpose and value-added contributions will evolve.* This means that it is necessary to check-in and review these elements periodically as your responsibilities change in your current role, and particularly if you change jobs or companies.

As long as you are engaged in the world of work, your Future-Proof Plan will be an ongoing work in progress. This inherent evolution does not suggest that you should waiver in your commitment to its requirements; rather, it should be considered a living and breathing document because you will inevitably learn, grow, and change with the changes you encounter. A Future-Proof Plan should also be dynamic enough to evolve with you as the relative priorities and areas of interest that hold your passion and focus shift.

TAKING THE SELF-ASSESSMENT—"HOW FUTURE-PROOF ARE YOU?"

Effective planning processes begin with an effort to assess the starting place and current context of *right now*. Appendix 1 includes a self-administered assessment that reveals how Future-Proof you are at the starting line. The eight questions provide a structured way to identify the match between your current attitudes, behaviors, and commitments with the indicators of Future-Proof behavior. If you take the ten-minute self-assessment now and then follow the suggestions that accompany your score, you will be fully prepared to implement the concepts in this chapter. Continue reading now if you choose to take the self-assessment at a later time.

VISUALIZING YOUR HORIZON—CREATING GOALS FOR YOUR WORKING LIFE

Setting and attaining goals is an intrinsic part of any career progression. Even people who are naturally averse to planning and prefer to just "let life come to them" often hold an intention or hope of some desired future. Visualizing your horizon is about developing a clear picture of what that hope is and then creating specific goals for your working life that reflect that intent. So, whether you are inclined to go with the flow, or interested in carefully mapping out the next several years or decades of your career, you need to have a sense of where you are heading if you ever hope to arrive there.

The important thing with *visualizing your horizon* is to describe the inner element of what it is you want, not the outer package it could potentially arrive in. For example, take this statement: "When I consider my future working life, I see a steady stream of promotions. Eventually my goal is to be a Vice President." You have just described the package that reflects the goal and, while promotions and titles may be important, truly defining the goal requires an expression of the inner picture, or *why it matters*. Consider this alternative statement: "When I consider my future working life, I see a steady stream of increasing challenges and responsibilities, which will culminate in a leadership role that allows me to significantly influence people and the direction of the company." What you have done here is express the important elements of the goal, without anchoring them to a specific package or set of circumstances.

Table 11.1   Visualizing Your Horizon and Creating Goals for Your Working Life

Visualizing the Horizon As you look into the future of your working life…	What specific opportunities, challenges, and successes do you hope to experience?	Without naming the specific outcomes (i.e., title, salary, etc.), what values and experiences are most important to you?	Based on how you see it now, what statement best describes the overall aspiration you have for your career and the quality of your working life?
Creating Goals for Your Working Life As you consider your starting place right now…	What elements of your purpose, contributions, and capabilities must be strengthened in order to attain the opportunities, challenges, and successes you hope to experience?	What potential actions do you need to consider to gain access to the specific values and experiences that are most important to you?	Considering your overall aspirations, what priorities and goals can you commit to right now in order to move closer toward the horizon?

The likelihood of creating the conditions where the first goal is reached is far less than the open-ended potential of the second one. If you frame the first goal as your horizon, is anything but a promotion to Vice President a failure? If you frame the second goal as your horizon, you could be Vice President, Director, or even CEO and still experience the most important aspects of the goal. Using the prompts in Table 11.1, chart a course toward your horizon by naming the goals and priorities you have for your working life.

MAP THE STRATEGY—PLOT A COURSE FOR THE WORKING LIFE YOU WANT

With your goals as motivation to push forward, the rest of this chapter will lead you through the process of mapping the remaining elements of your Future-Proof Plan. The four elements include: Clarifying Your Future-Proof Contributions; Refining Your Future-Proof Purpose; Identifying Your Future-Proof Capabilities;

and Establishing Your Future-Proof Relationships. After you complete these four exercises you can return to your horizon and goals in order to refine and integrate those within your completed plan.

CLARIFYING YOUR FUTURE-PROOF CONTRIBUTIONS

Two of the essential requirements for successfully navigating your hidden curriculum of work are identifying and delivering your *vital purpose* and *value-added contributions* at work consistently over time. Your capacity to do this sets you apart from other average contributors. And, in a time where average is over, adding value beyond your job description and delivering results in difficult situations can keep you ahead of the change curve and competitive in the job market.

The next step in creating your Future-Proof Plan is to refine and affirm your vital purpose and value-added contributions. If you completed the Six-Question Matrix in chapter 5, which is an exercise intended to dig below the SMW and reveal what you do that matters most to the team and organization, you have already started to identify your vital purpose and value-added contributions. Consider that product your "working draft" and use the next few sections to further refine and improve upon that starting place. To begin, you will look more closely at your contributions.

What is wrong with these statements? "I am a good people person." "I like to solve big problems." "I am an excellent communicator." "People rely on me because I just have a way of helping them think through things." "I am not afraid to call people on their stuff." "I just get things done." That was a trick question; there is nothing wrong with these statements—if you are in the SMW. These statements come from the responses of people I have coached through the process of seeing their "job-within-the-job." These are the first takes and initial responses to the question, *Which of your contributions have the greatest value to the organization?*

There really is no secret formula that will take you from these presenting, superficial statements to clear and precise definitions of your value-added contributions. It only requires a few repetitions to dig deeper, gain increasing insight, and express what you see in more concrete and specific terms. To make this clear, table 11.2 illustrates a juxtaposition of the initial statement and the finished version so you can see how the progression unfolded for my clients. Following this example there are multiple prompts that you can use to dig deeper on your own value-added contributions in table 11.3.

Table 11.2 Clarifying Value-Added Contributions

First-Take: Value-Added Contributions	Clarified: Value-Added Contributions
"I am a good people person."	"I take time to build rapport with the people I work with. This allows me to customize my approach to every interaction. This little bit of fore-thinking helps me avoid stepping on toes and in the end I am more persuasive."
"I like to solve big problems."	"My hand goes up when volunteers are needed for tough jobs. I thrive on the challenge, but more than that I am capable of taking a big-picture view and then breaking it down into manageable pieces."
"I am an excellent communicator."	"I understand that communication is so much more than the words I say and the way I listen to others. I always take time to read the room in order to adjust my interactions in a way that gets something productive done. When the tone is crisis-driven, I center myself and project a serious, but confident presence. When things are light, I join in so people know they can relate to me."
"People rely on me because I just have a way of helping them think through things."	"There is a unique perspective that comes with not getting involved in the petty politics at work. I have a way of rising above those, without projecting that I am *'better than them.'* When people are tired of the drama I am a go-to person that helps to refocus on the work at hand, including ways to separate the people from the issues."

Continued

Table 11.2 Continued

First-Take: Value-Added Contributions	Clarified: Value-Added Contributions
"I am not afraid to call people on their stuff."	"When the moment is right, I am not afraid to tell people that I disagree and think there is a better way. This is hard when it is your boss, but it is something that I can do without labeling things as right vs. wrong, triggering defenses, or causing a rift."
"I just get things done."	"I work harder than most people and my efforts go farther because I avoid distractions that can drain my energy. I don't flaunt it, but I let my boss and key colleagues know that things are delivered on time and above expectations."

Table 11.3 Clarify Your "Future-Proof Contributions"

First-Take: Value-Added Contributions	Clarified: Future-Proof Contributions
Contribution #1:	
Contribution #2:	
Contribution #3:	
Contribution #4:	
Contribution #5:	

A value-added contribution can be a single skill or attribute, though usually it comes together in a cluster of these things that are available to you in critical circumstances. That last part of the phrase is the key. If you are able to see the big picture and break it down into more manageable parts to get it done, then that is a value-added contribution for sure. However, if what is needed by the organization is someone who can do that in crisis-mode when things are high-pressured and ambiguous, it is not a value-added contribution if you can only deliver when you have time and predictability. Using the blank grid in Table 11.3, clarify your own top five Future-Proof contributions. You can start fresh, or begin by transferring your information from the Six-Question Matrix.

REFINING YOUR FUTURE-PROOF PURPOSE

Using these Future-Proof Contributions as incentive to stay on purpose, now you can look more deeply at the nature of your vital purpose. When you look at the Six-Question Matrix, you will notice that the vital purpose you hold is a direct reflection of the single statement that describes your "job." However, rather than just restating the superficial words from your job description, the statement that captures your vital purpose is a short, but powerful way to portray how your presence within the team and organization is *essential*.

When well-crafted, purpose statements serve as a source of inspiration, guidance, and discipline for you to stay focused on what matters most at work and they signal your contributions to others. Your actions will always have a greater effect than your words; however you can also use your purpose statement as a starting place to subtly brand yourself within the organization. In order to do this, you must go from purpose statement, to *Purpose Profile*.

My study of the changing world of work and the countless hours I have invested in helping people reveal and navigate their true challenges at work led me to develop Purpose Profiles, which reflect some of the most productive combinations of vital purpose, value-added contributions, and related hidden challenges to watch out for. While the goal of this section is not to provide an assessment that fits you into one or another type, table 11.4 illustrates the ways in which the factors come together to create relatable snapshots of the hidden curriculum of work.

After reading these Purpose Profiles, you will use the same framework to create your own in table 11.5. As you read through these examples, look for

Table 11.4 Purpose Profiles

Vital Purpose	Valued Contributions	Hidden Challenges
Catalyst "I make things happen when nobody else can."	Catalysts are the sparks that make things happen. They think in innovative ways and their actions ignite progress when pressure and resistance build. It may be a subtle insight, or a grand plan, but Catalysts have respect and use it to push ideas forward.	Bright, shiny objects can distract them from priorities and their impatience with structure can slow Catalysts down. At times they fail to ask enough of the right questions to identify important considerations and they can be unreliable. When there are uncommitted allies (Catalysts need Lookouts, Truth Tellers, and Systems Builders) their efforts to make change happen can easily stall.
Producer "I get the job done, no matter how difficult the task."	Producers crank out lots of good work. They are focused on seeing what is needed to keep progress going and they are skilled at following through on the delegation or completion of the tasks. Smart, critical thinkers, Producers can link strategy with execution effortlessly and although they prefer routine and structure, they remain flexible enough to adapt when needed.	Too much change in a short period of time can disrupt the cycle of implementation that Producers need, which can frustrate them and reduce the quality of their work. They can be impersonal at times and forget about the importance good relationships. They may get drained of energy and motivation so Producers work best when they have Motivators and Look Outs who can help them stay engaged and out in front of challenges.
Look Out "I make the critical observations, insights, and connections that keep us out of trouble."	Look Outs are watchful of risks, liabilities, and other bugaboos that could derail the show. They are compliance minded and they often ask hard questions that create pause for necessary consideration. They see	Look Outs can get tunnel vision, make decisions too quickly, or fixate on potential risks that are actually acceptable to take on. This can create pessimism, resistance, and road blocks that prevent progress and

Continued

Table 11.4 Continued

Vital Purpose	Valued Contributions	Hidden Challenges
	details that others may not, which enable them to make connections between opportunities and risks.	frustrate others. Look Outs are at their best when a strong Signal Caller can recognize their tendency to think one-dimensionally and re-direct their focus.
Truth Teller "I read the room and speak up at just the right time to say what needs to be said."	Truth Tellers see it like it is and say it like it is. The invaluable perspective they bring can reveal potentially dangerous gaps between ideas about what is possible and realities that limit it. When they speak their minds in ways that contribute positively, without offending people through excessive criticism, they help the team get to better results.	Truth Tellers sometimes believe they have the "only" truth and may fail to listen to others. Their advocacy for singular perspectives (often based on personal biases) can alienate people and limit the expression of diverse viewpoints that are needed for healthy discussion and well-tested decisions. To avoid bottlenecks, Truth Tellers need Catalysts who can respond to the facts and synthesize "Plan B" on the fly.
Signal Caller "I keep people on the same page so that we achieve the goals that matter."	Signal Callers are the quarterbacks that keep an eye on the coordination of roles and contributions. They are able to bring the best out of others because they understand that getting out of the way helps people stay on their vital purpose.	Signal Callers can get distracted by their coordination efforts and fail to deliver their own skills and abilities to the task at hand. When they experience personal or professional adversity or high-pressure situations, they can be reactive and have difficulty engaging with others consistently enough to keep things moving. Signal Callers need Systems Builders to create the structure for what needs to happen.

Systems Builder "I see the big picture, as well as the details required to put productive systems in place."	Systems Builders understand the structure and function of getting work done and they are able to translate ideas into action. They anticipate the mix of resources and capacity needed for producing high-quality outcomes and they have the ability to see important interfaces between details and the big picture.	Systems Builders can get caught up in the moving parts and minutiae of getting things done, which blocks their view of evolving conditions. Their dogged commitment to structure can sometimes lead to black/white thinking that gets them stuck when more creative problem solving could address issues successfully. Systems Builders need Foragers to ensure their resources are adequate and Look Outs to help them spot trouble with time to adjust the system before it is too late.
Forager "I connect people, ideas, and resources in surprising, innovative ways."	Foragers are resource magnets. They understand people and can spot talent when they see it. They are clever and creative and identify multiple options for achieving one goal.	Foragers can sometimes "wander off" and follow unnecessary leads that distract from urgent priorities. Their unpredictable nature can cause others to resist relying on them.
Motivator "I give people a reason to keep going and to remember why things matter when adversity strikes."	Motivators watch for opportunities to tap people's natural interests and get them aligned with their skills and potential contributions. They may be quiet, or they may be vocal in their efforts; either way they intuitively connect people with a bigger picture of what matters to draw them into a greater cycle of engagement and willingness to work through the challenges of change.	Motivators must be motivated themselves, so if their own intrinsic motivation and self-efficacy wane, they can withdraw. In their zeal, Motivators sometimes respond too quickly to the ideas of others and fail to develop a thorough approach based on a balanced assessment of the situation. Motivators sometimes miss the structural factors that potentially reduce motivation

Continued

Table 11.4 Continued

Vital Purpose	Valued Contributions	Hidden Challenges
		(i.e., performance and reward disconnects, etc.) and their efforts are not perceived as credible. A solid Catalyst is a great ally for a Motivator because their contributions build on each other.
Storyteller "I get people to understand and believe in something bigger than themselves."	Storytellers have a way of getting people on the same page by describing current scenarios and possible futures in ways that help people understand complex ideas. With powerful images, they translate the landscape around them in a way that encourages belief in what is possible. The connections between people and ideas that they communicate present a vision and a path forward that makes new initiatives more likely to succeed.	Storytellers can get captured by the drama and intrigue of their vision, which causes them to drift and overreach. They can get overly involved in work relationships at a personal level, which can lead to unchecked biases. Rather than communicating clearly, they sometimes emphasize the nuances and variations of a story in a way that confuses people and results in unclear options. Storytellers need Truth Tellers to ground their predictions and narratives and Motivators to buy-in and get others excited.

Table 11.5 Create Your Own Purpose Profile

Vital Purpose	Valued Contributions	Hidden Challenges
_____		

your own experiences reflected back and try to see yourself in several profiles. (Most Future-Proof people are dynamic and able to express different elements of multiple purposes based on what the situation requires.)

If you spotted yourself clearly in one or more example above, use that as a starting place to customize your own unique Purpose Profile. If you did not catch a glimpse of your unique combination of talent, experiences, and purpose in the examples above, use table 11.5 to create your own Purpose Profile from scratch. In column 1, try to name it with a headline and then draft a short, single-line description that captures the essence of your vital purpose. In columns 2–3 you can transfer the work you have already done on contributions and hidden challenges in this chapter (or from chapter 5's Six-Question Matrix and BLPA).

IDENTIFYING YOUR FUTURE-PROOF CAPABILITIES

In addition to staying on purpose and delivering value beyond your job description, the seminal capabilities of Future-Proof people in the world of work can be seen in their capacity to _"identify and transform barriers into opportunities for improved learning and performance...and make intentional adjustments in your attitude, knowledge, skills, and abilities to stay ahead of the change curve and remain relevant at work."_ This is the textbook definition of working in a Future-Proof way, however, when it gets down to where the rubber-meets-the-road, Future-Proof people are often fueled by a drive to:

- Develop the mental flexibility needed to adapt to constant change and ambiguity;
- Understand and solve complex problems through innovation;
- Identify clear learning goals associated with their highest priorities;
- Elevate their personal energy and motivation for continuous growth;
- Seek and respond to feedback;

- Stay persistent through challenges and remain resilient in the face of adversity;
- Maintain integrity and respect for themselves and others; and
- Leverage the connection between individual performance, team contribution, and organizational impact.

In addition to these values and drivers, Future-Proof people also possess four common skills, including the ability to

- Recognize priorities, then follow through on them to make an impact;
- Relate to and collaborate well with others when it counts;
- Communicate a point of view to generate compelling ideas; and
- Learn to make creative connections by synthesizing diverse, contradictory ideas.

These four unique skill sets, or capabilities, help Future-Proof people respond to the challenges and demands they face in the world of work. Often referred to as "soft skills," because they are not based on technical expertise, capabilities like these are anything but "soft" in the sense of importance. They are skills that help people successfully respond to complex, challenging situations. In order for you to establish a Future-Proof plan you need to assess the need for and develop certain core capabilities that work for you.

The unique application of these skill sets varies based on your personality and the demands of your working life, though some of the essentials are the same for most people. In table 11.7 you will complete a capabilities assessment called The Seventh Question. This will allow you to draw upon your vital purpose and value-added contributions in order to establish a baseline need of the capabilities required to deliver them consistently. In order to give you insight into the difference between a vaguely described "skill" and a well-directed "Future-Proof Capability," here are four common, but indispensible capabilities, of Future-Proof people.

#1 – FUTURE-PROOF CHANGE

The Concept: Change affects the bottom, middle, and top of every organization. It is no longer an option to simply relegate responses to change to the people in an organization who are formally labeled as "leaders." Future-Proof people understand that they are leaders (guiding themselves and inspiring others) at

Figure 11.1 CG^2 – A Model for Future-Proof Change Management.

every level of the organization chart. Everyday leaders who are engaged and active follow three fundamental steps to successfully manage change. They know their *context*, define clear *goals*, and manage the *gaps* between goals and obstacles.

The Practice: The image in figure 11.1 illustrates the way in which Future-Proof people manage themselves and influence others by understanding context, defining goals, and managing gaps.

The Result: Integrating the CG^2 sequence will help you understand your circumstances in periods of heightened ambiguity and change. With this progression as a guide you can learn to evolve with change, without becoming collateral damage to its shifting priorities and contradictions. As you anticipate changes in the environment more fluidly and determine priorities more efficiently, you will increase your capacity for innovation. Ultimately this will make you better at inventing your own work and adding increased value. Finally, the process will increase your resilience as you confidently address gaps and obstacles as they emerge.

#2 – FUTURE-PROOF COLLABORATION

The Concept: Future-Proof people know that great things are seldom accomplished alone. While it is true that most of them rely on and actively exercise their intuition, wisdom, and sense of purpose at a personal level, they also understand that partnering with others is an essential ingredient of accomplishing large-scale change. However, Future-Proof people are selective and disciplined when it comes to when, how, and with whom they will collaborate. They engage in Future-Proof collaboration, which is *intentional partnering that maximizes the chance of success by aligning the needed strategic skill or resource with the essential contributors in the most efficient way.*

The Practice: Not all collaboration succeeds, and so instead of relying on partnerships and contributions from others that are dictated by circumstance and opportunity, Future-Proof people deliberately seek out Future-Proof collaboration opportunities that serve a specific purpose and match their highest priority in the moment. Sometimes the missing piece is motivation, and that can be found through a partnership with some individual or group who is driven, focused, and inspired. At other times the missing piece may be technical, strategic, or organizational. In these instances the mix of skills, abilities, and access to resources serves as the driver for Future-Proof collaboration. There is reciprocity with this as well. Future-Proof people are often invited to collaborate with others and they accept these invitations *only* when the best mix of skill and contribution can be aligned in an effective way. They are not selective because they "have better things to do;" they choose the moments where their impact can be the greatest.

The Result: Learning how to exercise Future-Proof collaboration will help you take advantage of a hyperconnected world and use collaboration as a tool to accomplish things that otherwise would not be feasible alone. The discipline of selective collaboration allows you to avoid wasting time when collaboration is a substitute for lack of creativity, vision, or accountability for individual follow-through.

#3 – FUTURE-PROOF COMMUNICATION

The Concept: Future-Proof people create their own possibilities through communication. They understand that communication is not improved simply by being more assertive, picking your words more carefully, or having scripted conversations for difficult encounters. Future-Proof people understand and recognize that communication is generative—it makes things. And they deliberately make the patterns of communication, interaction, and relationships that help them to bring their purpose and value-added contributions closer to reality.

The Practice: Future-Proof people instinctively focus on communication in this multidimensional way because they understand that the meaning and results of their experience are a reflection of the quality of our patterns of interaction with others. For example, strong advocacy for ideas can create a pattern of alienation. Fear of change and overly conservative responses to new ideas can lead to a pattern of entrenchment and avoidance. Whatever the situation,

Future-Proof people know they can make and remake unwanted experiences and outcomes in ways that create alternative patterns for preferred interactions and outcomes.[1]

Making possibilities through communication is more than exercising charisma, charm, or other positive relational traits. While it is true that Future-Proof people often exude confidence and can generate quick rapport with diverse people, they are also patient because they understand that it is the everyday interactions that ultimately shape our patterns of communication over time. Among other things, Future-Proof people use communication to start productive habits. For example, when there is an important meeting and a decision will be made about a critical endeavor, Future-Proof people instinctively use communication to make hidden values, fears, and priorities visible and discussible or to share their highest hopes and priorities in a way that can be contrasted with others. This provides the opportunity for honest conversation about the factors involved in discussions, decisions, and key actions.

The Result: Future-Proof communication will help you to remake unwanted patterns of communication and interaction with others and to transform those into stronger relationships. Using these preferred patterns allows you to create organizational cultures that establish the conditions necessary to achieve your important priorities and ultimately add increasing value.

#4 – FUTURE-PROOF CREATIVITY

The Concept: Future-Proof people find intersections of creativity that draw inspiration from multiple perspectives and unexpected places. These intersections are potentially everywhere in a hyperconnected world, and the nexus of creativity that they can create leads to a virtuous cycle and multiplier effect of new insights.

The Practice: Future-Proof people take this inspiration from unlikely places and then formulate breakthrough ideas and more creative insights. With the abundance of fresh and meaningful sources of creativity, Future-Proof people use time as a tool. They can leverage a visit to the art museum to inspire new ways of approaching noncreative dilemmas, and they can use a mundane task like ordering a meal to discover creative approaches to enhancing ideas about customer service. You may have heard the saying that "there are not enough hours in the day" to get things done: Future-Proof people do not face this problem, because their pursuits are often layered so tightly that they never pursue just one single endeavor. All parts work in parallel toward the whole to build something bigger and better.

The Result: Finding intersections of creativity will help you to pursue break-through ideas by nurturing the natural, dynamic patterns and connections that show up across different disciplines and industries. Leaner and more agile approaches to innovation often come in unexpected packages and the ability to spot these and imagine new and different applications can lead to surprising ways of adding value.

ESTABLISHING YOUR FUTURE-PROOF RELATIONSHIPS

You have now completed three of the major elements of your Future-Proof Plan. So far, all of your efforts have been focused inwardly and now it is time to look outside of yourself at the relationships in your world of work. No person is an island and achieving the goals you have for a long, successful working life require supportive relationships along the way. In chapter 5 you explored your "job-within-the-job" in Three Dimensions, which allowed you to scan up, down, and across the organization to see the reporting relationships and team collaborators that are vital to your success. Building on that effort, you are going to use the prompts in table 11.6 to create a kind of map that clarifies the full range of supportive relationships you need to achieve your goals. These can be people you work with, report to, or simply seek out as mentors along the way. (If you do not assess the quality of relationships you have, you will not know how you need to fine-tune them or let them go in order to create the mix you need.)

To begin, consider the variety of relationships you already engage in at the critical interfaces of your working life. As you go through the Relationship Mapping Exercise, use the prompts to think about the specific people who already know and support you, as well as those who need to know and support you more. As with any relationship, the foundation is based on mutual respect and investment—so for every person who may do something that helps you, imagine how you could reciprocate.

THE SEVENTH QUESTION

Now that you have reviewed the brief descriptions of these four Future-Proof capabilities you have a better idea of the ways in which strengths, skills, and abilities become core assets in your Future-Proof Plan. There is a Seventh Question

Table 11.6 Future-Proof Relationship Map

Future-Proof Plan	Who Are They?	What Do They Do?	Who Do You Need?
Goals	Do you have at least two people in your working life who understand your horizon, including the specific goals that you hope to experience in your working life? Who are they?	If yes, how clearly do they understand what matters to you, and how active are they in helping you achieve your goals?	If no, is there someone you know who could potentially appreciate your working life goals and get behind you in support? How will you reach out to them?
Vital Purpose	Do you have somebody in your working life who understands your vital purpose and believes in its significance? Who is it?	If yes, how active are they in helping you achieve your working life goals and stay on purpose?	If no, is there somebody with whom you could share to potentially gain their confidence and belief in your vital purpose?
Value-Added Contributions	Do you have at least three people in your working life who understand your value-added contributions and recognize their impact? Who are they?	If yes, how actively do they advocate on your behalf of your contributions to others? Are they in positions of influence?	If no, are there people you could share with to potentially gain their confidence in the reach/value of your contributions?
Capabilities	Do you have at least four people in your working life who possess the capabilities that you seek? Who are they?	If yes, are you able to observe and learn from these people to see how they apply their capabilities on the job? Can you reach out to them for feedback and support to cultivate your own practice?	If no, how will you identify positive role models that you can learn from and push yourself to grow?

that has been deliberately left out of the Six-Question Matrix that can help you identify your own Future-Proof capabilities. The question is the next obvious progression in the process; however, it was excluded in chapter 5 because of the value of handling it separately from the others. The missing question is: *What skills are required for me to stay on purpose, consistently deliver my value-added contributions, and successfully navigate the challenges of my hidden curriculum of work?*

This is a critical question because it implies that simply seeing the hidden side of work is not enough; a new range of measures to meet its challenges is also required. Much of this book has argued that the greatest *ability* lies is in the capacity to look at work through the lens of the hidden curriculum. While this is true, there are additional tools and skills people need to address their true challenges of work.

The goal of this exercise is to respond to the Seventh Question. To begin, use the three-column exercise in table 11.7 to transfer the specific elements of your vital purpose and value-added contributions. Place the list in column 1, and then name the associated talent or skill required to deliver it in column 2. You can draw upon the descriptions of the Purpose Profiles or of the four Future-Proof Capabilities described in the last section. These all hold clues about the essential skills and abilities that your hidden curriculum of work demands

Table 11.7   Future-Proof Capabilities

Purpose/Contribution	Required Skill to Deliver	Current Capacity
Example: "I contribute a clear voice and decisive perspective to our team meetings."	*Example:* "I have to stay present in the critical conversations, discern the most important issues, and articulate the choices we have. At the same time I cannot let my emotions cloud my objectivity."	1 **2** 3 4 5

from you. In column 3 you can indicate your current capacity on a scale of #1–5 (1 = unable to consistently and effectively deliver the purpose/value and 5 = able to consistently and effectively deliver the purpose/value). For anything that is ranked #1–3, you need to brainstorm practical target areas below to grow and increase capacity.

PUTTING YOUR FUTURE-PROOF PLAN INTO ACTION

You now have the ingredients to assemble your Future-Proof Plan and put it into action. The process of creating your Future-Proof Plan was about clearly stating what hopes and goals inspire and drive you (your horizon and goals), why you do what you do and what makes you indispensible (your purpose), what you bring to the table to help yourself and others succeed (your value-added contributions), and who understands what matters to you and can help you achieve your goals (your relationships).

The exciting part of this process is that you have many very practical starting places to implement your plan. If you want to begin really slowly, simply revisit the results from your Self-Assessment—"How Future-Proof Are You?"—and follow those recommendations. For a more aggressive starting place, you can delve into your Future-Proof Purpose and Value-Added Contributions and consider ways to deliver those more consistently and effectively. This can include a review of your current assignments and subsequent action planning to determine where potential gaps are or could be that may undermine your best work.

If you are experiencing a troubled relationship at work, you can begin by referring to the Relationship Mapping Exercise you just completed to look more comprehensively at whether the relationship fits into your priorities and needs. In some instances you may be able to let some old relationships go, while in other cases you may want to invest more time and energy into creating a more mutually supportive connection.

Wherever you begin is where you are. And, as you move along your path to go *beyond the job description* and achieve *breakthrough performance*, you will accomplish goals that bring you closer to your horizon. This gives you the opportunity to update your plan with new goals that stretch you even further. If your job or career changes and another iteration of purpose, contribution, and capability is required, you can update your Future-Proof Plan as the conditions evolve.

KEY TAKEAWAYS

To take the driver's seat in your working life you need a Future-Proof Plan that integrates your everyday efforts to navigate the hidden curriculum of work and your long-term career development that will shape the working life you want. The three steps to create your customized Future-Proof Plan are to (1) *Take the Self-Assessment—"How Future-Proof Are You?"*; (2) *Visualize Your Horizon—Create Goals for Your Working Life; and* (3) *Map the Strategy—Plot a Course for the Working Life You Want.* Using the prompts and activities provided will bring your Future-Proof Plan to life in a way that it evolves with you as you move through your working life.

Chapter 12

YOUR DAILY COMPASS FOR SOLO NAVIGATION

WE MAKE OUR OWN EXPERIENCE at work. Regardless of our title, tenure, or slot on the organization chart, *we* are the single greatest influence that shapes the quality and character of our working lives. This gives us tremendous power—especially if we are unhappy with our job, the quality of our work, or the prospect of what lies ahead on the horizon; *we can* make something better. This means that we have a personal responsibility for translating our unsatisfying experiences in the workplace into more enjoyable experiences with better outcomes. The purpose of this chapter is to provide you with a daily compass for your solo navigation. This can help you stay on track with your Future-Proof Plan and it can give you the "shot in the arm" you need if the hidden curriculum of work overwhelms you.

Forget about your team and the larger organization, at least for now. This is about *your* True North and the action steps you can take to invest in what you need to stay on your path to success. Figure 12.1 offers a picture of your *Daily Compass for Solo Navigation,* including a description of each cardinal direction.

NORTH

Your North Star is the intersection of your vital purpose, value-added contributions, and hidden challenges. Your true challenges of work are reflected in this equation:

Vital Purpose + Value-Added Contributions + Hidden Challenges = "Job-within-the-Job"

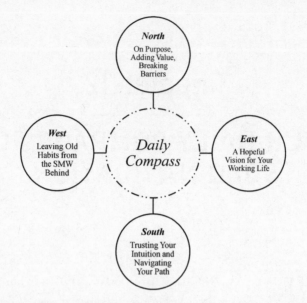

Figure 12.1   Daily Compass for Solo Navigation.

However, your ongoing performance and the state of your working life can be measured by this revised equation:

On Purpose + Adding Value – Unresolved Challenges = Future-Proof Capacity

If you get off purpose, fail to consistently deliver your best contributions, or get overrun by your hidden challenges, the barriers to learning and performance within your "job-within-the-job" will break you down and potentially put you at risk of being left behind. Alternatively, if you are on purpose, adding value, and navigating your challenges, then your Future-Proof competence will rise, giving you the best chance to stand out from the competition, stay ahead of the change curve, and craft a long and successful working life that matches your deepest values and highest aspirations.

Knowing that there will always be bad days and teachable moments we wish we could have back, the most important thing you can do to get Future-Proofed and stay on your path to success at work is to keep your True North in front of you. Here are three daily questions you should ask yourself when facing North:

- *What vital purpose can I play today?*
- *What value-added contributions can I deliver during my key interactions today?*
- *What challenges could surface and interfere with my best work today?*

EAST

One of the most important things you can do every day is to reset your mental balance as you interpret the challenges that lie ahead of you and the reasons you can confidently believe in your capacity to meet their demands. If you have a hopeful vision for the working life you want, then that can provide you with the drive, motivation, and commitment to move ahead. The incline of the hidden curriculum of work is steep, but after reading this book you now have tools for that climb.

Every challenge holds a kernel of insight into what is needed for you to succeed. As you process the experience of each day, try to notice the opportunity embedded within each challenge and use that insight to push your contribution into directions that bring you closer to your hopeful vision. There are no shortcuts to the working life you want, but noticing the opportunity within each challenge can serve as a milestone to accelerate the journey. Here are three daily questions you should ask yourself when facing East:

- *What specific elements of my working life can I strive toward today?*
- *What aspects of my current situation are unwanted and ripe for remaking?*
- *What is the first move I can make so that today is a true step toward my priorities?*

SOUTH

If the key to becoming Future-Proof is to add increasing value to the organization, it stands to reason that a curious and active mind is the starting place for success. Since you have to invent your own work to some degree (i.e., be self-initiating, lead with your own vision of priorities, trust your intuition, etc.), you need an intense curiosity about what would make things better. Riding the slipstream of your own curiosity and belief in *the big picture of what matters* is a reminder that—even on days when your tasks and activities feel full of busy-work—it is all just part of your effort to double down on your own investment in *your* future success.

The daily practice here is to stay mindful of the fact that you are navigating a path with no end. While that statement could feel exhausting, it does not have to be. Although the path to success at work winds until we exit the workforce in retirement, we can bring considerably more predictability around the conditions of success in our working lives when we go *Beyond the Job Description.*

This means that our natural tendency to seek a plateau needs to be guarded against. Rather than falling into new routines and staying satisfied with what those bring, we have to remember that even those habits will be challenged by evolving circumstances as the world of work continues to spin. Here are three daily questions you should ask yourself when facing South:

- *What recent experiences (challenges/successes) can I learn from?*
- *In what ways can I rely more on my own intuition and gut instincts?*
- *Thinking about recent outcomes that went bad, in what way did I tune out that inner voice and lose track of my big picture priorities?*

WEST

Looking West reminds you that what has worked in the past, including some of the most comfortable habits of the SMW, may need to sunset. Letting go of existing routines can be difficult, but staying Future-Proof requires continuous evaluation of the true challenges of work and a steady focus on what is needed to succeed as conditions change. It is important to remember that, prior to revealing your "job-within-the-job," your sense of priorities and the choices you made about how to invest time and energy at work were not focused on *you*. In the SMW, your time and energy was focused on the tasks and activities that drained your time, as well as the nagging challenges from the hidden side of work that were always felt, but never fully seen.

With a clearer picture of your vital purpose, value-added contributions, and potential challenges, you must reevaluate the way you think about your day. When the changes you need to pursue represent a marked departure from the SMW (and/or from the way others around you work), it takes courage and foresight to make the move. It is okay to start slowly, but movement is the key. The plateau-mentality often creeps up after a wave of progress, so you need to fight through that tendency of accepting progress that feels "good enough." Here are three daily questions you should ask yourself when facing West:

- *What elements of the SMW could distract me today?*
- *What can I stop doing in order to stay on purpose, add value, and expose my challenges?*
- *In what ways can I proactively communicate what I am doing so that others will support it?*

THE POWER OF NOTICING

The hidden curriculum of work is everywhere, all the time. The trick is being able to spot it accurately and see it for what it truly demands. Your Future-Proof Plan and your Daily Compass for Solo Navigation have clarified your hidden curriculum of work in greater detail and they provide an action plan for navigating its challenges. In order to assist you further with the capacity to "see" the hidden side of work, the remainder of this chapter is devoted to sharpening your ability to notice what is all around you.

The most important skill you need moving forward is the power to notice how and when your hidden curriculum surfaces so that your Future-Proof Plan can take effect. Noticing is the most disruptive thing you can do. It offers an elegant disintegration of our expectations so that the stuff we *expect to see* can be replaced by *a new perspective* of what is possible.

What is required to move from observing to taking focused action for change is the hard-earned *objective flexibility* that only comes from the power of noticing. An observer's mind will create awareness, and this awareness is *the* energetic catalyst for change and a key to performance improvement of all types. I often share a simple formula with my coaching clients, which represents this progression: *Awareness of Barriers + On-Going Focused Attention = Pathway to Improved Learning & Performance.*

Some people object to this equation because they recognize that it is missing an important component: the intervention. I explain that the intervention is actually secondary because it is only until we begin to develop an awareness of barriers and place ongoing focused attention on their influence that we then make it possible to resolve them. In other words, the intervention is critical, but efforts to reduce the impact of barriers will be ineffective unless the barrier itself is deeply understood. If this equation is achieved, then rather than sustaining a barrier's silent, but powerful influence on us, we put ourselves in a position to dictate its future impact. Until then, we do not truly have a barrier; *it* has us. Here are six daily reminders to help you deeply notice the hidden curriculum of work and use your Daily Compass wisely:

Get Curious, Stay Curious

Imagine yourself exploring the "what and why" about things without judging or concluding too much about whether they are *good* or *bad*. This spark of curiosity by nature is not judgmental, so it does not get deterred by feelings of discouragement or self-doubt. Asking "What and why" and following up with questions like "Why does that matter?" and "What is that creating?" can lead to a deep and increasingly healthy inquiry that reveals the inner dynamics of barriers and their impact.

Allow Things to be Revealed

As you explore and notice barriers, strike the balance between the *finesse of revealing* and the *force of discovering* what is present. The deeper insights are revealed when we let them surface, rather than forcing things that potentially trigger defensive reactions.

Read Your Own Body Language

If we take a beginner's mind and really pay attention, then our own somatic processes (e.g., presence, posture, nonverbal communication, etc.) can show us a lot of what our brains will not. Recognizing our own *facial misbehavior* when we hear a certain comment or noticing that we start *twisting in our seats* when we're uncomfortable are just two examples of clues that something important or sensitive is present just below the reaction.

Look for the Underlying Dynamic

There is always much more going on below the surface than we can see. Focusing on the underlying root issues, values, meanings, and interests can widen our perspectives. If we simply take the presenting problem for granted, we will often "solve the wrong problem" and miss the core barrier.

Expect to See the Unexpected

When we challenge (and remind) ourselves to expect to see something new and different, we free our patterns of quick assumption making and put ourselves in a position to recognize and respond to new possibilities. Much has been written about the danger of assumptions, and it can be summarized like this: we will see what we expect to see. To avoid the imposed limits of confirmation bias,[1] which hurts our learning and growth, we have to literally expect to see something new.

Muster Urgency in the Critical Moment

The critical moment is the instant of recognition when a specific attitude or behavior is reflected back to us and we see the barrier for what it is. Our *next response* in that instant marks a significant turn in how things unfold from there. The moment tends to pass quickly, and if we do not pay attention, our responses can be knee-jerk reactions fueled by habit and a strong sense of how we "ought to respond" based on prior interpretations of similar situations. If we want to shift and make something different, it is up to us to seize the moment by channeling a sense of energy and urgency. This will provide a motivational foundation to pursue a deeper understanding of the barrier and its underlying dynamics, to which is necessary to respond wisely.

Collectively, these suggestions serve as a commitment to become aware of the inner attitudes, behaviors, and decision-making processes that guide you. Because awareness is the key to making any change, we have to keep an observer's eye in order to steadily examine and learn from what we notice.

KEY TAKEAWAYS

We make our own experience at work. Regardless of our title, tenure, or slot on the organization chart, *we* ultimately are the greatest influence that shapes the quality of our working lives. This gives us tremendous power when we are unhappy with our job, the quality of our work, or the prospect of what lies ahead on the horizon because *we can* make something better. There is a daily compass that you can use to support your solo navigation and it provides a clear picture of your True North and the action steps you can take to invest in what is needed to stay on your path to success.

Your North Star is the intersection of your vital purpose, value-added contributions, and hidden challenges. Looking East, there is a hopeful vision for your working life that inspires your effort and draws you toward that desired future. Facing South, you have cues to trust your intuition and continue navigating along your path. And facing West reminds you to let go of old habits and acknowledge the full range of challenges and opportunities presented by the hidden curriculum of work.

The four cardinal directions act as a metaphor to help you orient yourself daily and stay on your path to success at work. The questions that reflect the demands of each direction can act as reminders to continue doing what is needed in your daily work to go *beyond the job description* and achieve *breakthrough performance*. Once you practice these cardinal directions, your daily compass will give you an effective way to cultivate a Future-Proof mind-set.

With your Daily Compass as a guide, *noticing* opportunities to navigate the hidden curriculum of work is the most disruptive thing you can do. It offers an elegant disintegration of your expectations so that *new perspectives* are possible. What is required to move from observing to taking focused action for change is the hard-earned *objective flexibility* that only comes from the power of noticing. An observer's mind will create awareness, and this awareness is *the* energetic catalyst for change and a key to performance improvement of all types.

Chapter 13

A GUIDE TO TEAM NAVIGATION

NAVIGATING THE HIDDEN CURRICULUM OF work is both an individual and a team pursuit. At the surface level, you might think that individual navigation is more straightforward than team efforts because you only address a single "job-within-the-job" and its interfaces. Alternatively, you could assume that a team process is more complex because you have to respond to a variety of intersecting challenges and personalities within the mix. In my experience there are challenges and opportunities with each, and labeling one "easy" and the other "difficult" is unhelpful.

As an individual you have a simpler picture to address, but you also have your own legacy of blind spots and limits in thinking to contend with. And, while it is more complicated to address intersecting concerns and the mixed motivations of people working through shared challenges, the benefit of multiple perspectives and the mix of strengths can be an asset. Either way, both approaches need to be in your repertoire. You have already learned how to respond to your individual hidden curriculum of work. The purpose of this chapter is to provide you with an easy-to-use guide for team navigation.

Like most innovations or change efforts, it is often just one or two individuals within a team that serve as the catalyst(s) for bringing new insights that spark the change. If you are that person and hope to inspire or lead your team to effectively meet the demands of the hidden side of work, then these starting lines will give you ideas for the design and scripting needed to kick-off your effort. The reality is that most challenging barriers will undoubtedly involve others and so you will want to learn ways to collaborate with team members to resolve a variety of workplace headaches that affect more than just you. Here are some tips for making Nav-Maps with teams Before, During, and After the issue(s) surface.

BEFORE

In the optimal scenario, a few ingredients will already be in place to make it easier to address the hidden curriculum of work. These include a supportive environment where people can speak freely, a willingness to listen to different perspectives, and a commitment to investing time and energy into creating a better way to work. If these ingredients are present, then less set-up is required. If they are not present or are felt inconsistently, then your first move is to create a *specific invitation* that sets up a conversation with this tone:

> "I would like to invite you to a short meeting to explore options to help us address some of our recent challenges. It will be short and sweet, because I know how valuable everyone's time is. The goal is to brainstorm alternative ways of thinking about the issue so that we can potentially turn this situation into an opportunity for growth and improvement. We have a flexible agenda that will get everyone involved, so it definitely will not be a boring meeting."

If you are unable to get buy-in with others or if time pressures prevent you from getting a response to the invitation, do not wait. You can always start the Nav-Map yourself and look for an opening in the future. If you have already started to work through the issue on your own, the invitation shifts to something like this:

"Can we find some time to meet in the next day or so? I have been working on some challenges and I have a couple of ideas that I want to run by you and get your perspective...when are you available?"

DURING

Once you arrive for the session, do not overcomplicate things with lofty descriptions or process steps. Have blank Nav-Map templates for everyone ready, as well as copies of the BLPA if there is a need to identify and explore possible core barriers. During the session, the agenda could include steps like these that you tailor to the specific personality of the team:

1. "We all bump into obstacles at work. Our recent struggles give us an opportunity to address them proactively. I'd like us to try a different approach to getting down to the core issues to find out if we can turn them into an opportunity for positive change."
2. "Let's start by getting a clearer picture of what each of us thinks is going on. Please write down the 2–3 greatest challenges you feel our team is facing (or take this quick BLP Assessment to identify core barriers)."
3. "Alright, now let's spend a few minutes talking about them until we get one that feels relevant to everyone to some degree."
4. "Now that we have a "core barrier" that we agree is causing our challenges, let's take it through a 4-part process."
5. Complete the Constellation exercise and discuss questions like: *"What did we expose here?"*
6. Complete the VPB exercise and discuss questions like: *"In what ways are our views matching or diverging?"*
7. Complete the Trip-Wire Pattern exercise and discuss questions like: *"What seems to be the moment of truth where we keep repeating the pattern?"*
8. Complete the Action Continuum exercise and discuss questions like: *"What commitment will be required to start moving along the continuum to achieve these action steps?"*

Note: If things feel forced at all during steps 5–7, take a break and regroup. If things stall, you might need to put a different barrier in the core because it is possible that you do not have the true, core issue identified. If things flow well, then move through the final step and take advantage of your momentum for problem solving.

AFTER

If the work feels finished, then move onto the next navigation opportunity. If the work is unfinished, or if people struggle in any way but remain willing to keep at it, then schedule another session a few days later. Keep the open-minded, light attitude to take pressure off of the concept of "doing this right." Invite other people to lead the next session(s) so that they are pushed to learn the steps and integrate the sequence.

If people are overmatched by the challenges, or if they are unwilling to keep at it for other reasons, continue solo navigation and model the application of the *Beyond the Job Description* insights and tools to show a better way of working. They may come around in the future.

If people find value in Nav-Maps and get curious, use the opening to share the concept of getting Future-Proofed with them. Invite them (and other key influencers) to understand more about the hidden side of work and share examples of the various ways to establish a culture of continuous learning and performance (the "E" in the R-I-T-E Model) in chapter 15.

KEY TAKEAWAYS

Navigating the hidden curriculum of work is both an individual and a team pursuit. Although it may seem simpler to navigate challenges from a single "job-within-the-job" at the individual level, team navigation processes hold potential for big breakthroughs. There are specific actions that you can take before, during, and after meetings with colleagues to effectively facilitate team Nav-Map sessions. All of the cues suggested in the sample timeline offer a flexible model to address people where they are and to prioritize the value of Nav-Maps over the process steps to make them.

Chapter 14

MANAGING TO THE HIDDEN SIDE OF WORK

MANAGING IS A CHALLENGE IN any environment. Even when you know what your employees' true priorities, opportunities, and challenges are, it can be difficult to establish expectations and accountabilities and sustain the ongoing conversations required to support their performance over time. However, managing the true challenges of work with the mind-set of the SMW creates an impossible situation.

When your orientation to work flows through the SMW, your approach to management is based on a superficial understanding of the true demands of your employees' work. This limited perspective can reduce your managerial moves to a *distraction* at worst, and at best, a mere band-aid that temporarily improves the presenting conditions for the employee, but fails to be a catalyst for doing great work. Over time this approach can also erode the credibility that the manager has with the direct report.

In order to unleash your team's potential and address the root-cause performance gaps that stand in the way of their best work, you must manage to the hidden side of work. This chapter provides a crash course on the day-to-day shifts leaders can make to go from managing the SMW to managing the hidden curriculum of work.

LESS IS MORE

A general rule of thumb in management is: *less is always more*. Good managers seldom implement a lot of different interventions; in fact they often focus on only a few priorities that can make the biggest difference for their people. Once they understand what these are, they invest in getting them right, which is as much about saying "no" to other distractions as it is about executing the tactics that will lead to the changes they seek. If you have ever worked for a boss who managed by the "flavor-of-the-month" rule, then you know how exhausting it is to be on the receiving end of a steady stream of new approaches that amount to little more than rearranging the deck chairs on the Titanic. Managing to the hidden side of work provides the constraints needed to focus on just a few domains, each of which has significant potential to support the increased learning and performance of others.

FOCUS ON VALUE, NOT STUFF

Sometimes managers get really good at providing basic administrative supports to their people. For example, your manager could spend considerable time handling clerical and organizational functions that make your work easier. These could include introducing new processes and programs, procuring resources, managing budget requests, approving time off, generating opportunities for training and development, and advocating for you and the rest of the team with other departments. In some cases these things are helpful, but they are not the most valuable. However, when managers invest time in understanding their employee's genuine concerns and deliver relevant managerial interventions that solve problems and remove roadblocks to getting great work done, they become a critical link in the performance chain.

Managing to the employee's ultimate concern generates tremendous respect within the reporting relationship. And, if managers also bring *Beyond the Job Description* tools (i.e., knowledge and experience to turn their everyday challenges into opportunities for improved learning and performance), that respect can elevate to true added value.

> Based on the philosophies of "Less Is More" and "Focus on Value, Not Stuff," this is the brass-knuckles definition of effective management: helping people understand and transform the everyday challenges that prevent their best work—then getting out of the way!

I am not suggesting that managers should abandon the general roles and functions they play within their organizations. As I said, many of these things are necessary and helpful. However, if more managers adopted this simple definition of management, and subsequently invested more of their time and energy in their efforts to expose the hidden challenges their teams face and deliver effective tools to address those challenges, it would improve the performance and productivity of not just the individuals within the team, but also within the organization overall. For managers to extend the competencies of *Beyond the Job Description,* they need an understanding of the specific management practices that respond to the hidden curriculum of work. The following framework teaches both emerging and established leaders the relevant components required to manage in this alternative way.

SPECIFIC MANAGEMENT PRACTICES IN THE HIDDEN CURRICULUM OF WORK

If the driving purpose of a manager is to *help their people understand and transform the everyday challenges that prevent them from doing their best work,* then the way that purpose is met is through the following seven commitments and practices:

1. Establish a supportive, trust-based relationship that places the quality of the employee's working life at the center of importance;[1]
2. Accurately assess the individual's knowledge, skills, and abilities in relation to the requirements of meeting the true demands of their "job-within-the-job;"
3. Work with the employee to define the mutually beneficial agenda, where their vital purpose, value-added contributions, and career aspirations align with the needs of the team and the overall goals of the organization;
4. Create expectations about communication, collaboration, and performance early and reinforce them often;
5. Make the hidden side of work continuously discussible and invest time and resources into others' processes of refining their "job-within-the-job" as conditions change;
6. Stay present enough to observe their success, as well as gaps in their on-going progress; and
7. Communicate early and often when expectations and accountabilities go unmet.

Beyond these seven commitments and practices, the best way to supervise effectively is to hire effectively. Once a person is hired, the best way to supervise effectively is to stay engaged with them in regular conversation about their performance. This means sharing honest feedback in real-time. Staying in regular conversation with team members in this way has many benefits, including:

- Improved clarity and focus about priorities and expectations;
- Faster identification and removal of barriers;
- Improved communication and better mutual trust/cooperation;
- Quicker completion of projects/tasks; and
- Increased investment and ownership on the part of the employee.

STRUCTURING EVERYDAY COMMUNICATION

Managers have to initiate clear, honest, and consistent communication through 1:1 conversations. Laissez-faire attitudes that managers sometimes cloak in the falsely positive desires to "let others lead" and to "avoid micro-managing" need to be replaced with earnest commitment to getting in the trenches to help others succeed. Good 1:1 conversations are private, focused discussions that highlight the unique challenges/opportunities of the direct report. Here are a few rules of thumb when leading 1:1s:

- Know your direct reports "job-within-the-job" (if you don't have a clue, how can you help them meet its demands?);
- Set expectations and measure performance based on their "job-within-the-job," not just their standard position description;
- Meet as often as it is useful and only as long as necessary;
- Schedule 1:1's for a regular time/day each week/month and keep to the schedule;
- Establish a regular agenda with time for open topics;
- Empower the employee to co-develop the agendas for on-going 1:1 meetings so they develop capacity to advocate for the specific support they need;
- Come to the meetings prepared with relevant information and feedback (don't wing it); and
- Take notes and send follow-up e-mails confirming what was agreed upon and what must happen between meetings.

MANAGE RELATIONSHIPS WHERE THEY ARE,
NOT WHERE YOU WISH THEY WERE

The regime of 1:1 meetings that you establish is important because it becomes the connective tissue that keeps your finger on the pulse of what is happening with your team. The key to success for these ongoing meetings is talking openly and honestly about what you see, not *what you hope to see.* This also happens to be a critical success factor for management in general. By extension, we have to manage the people we have, not the ones we wish we had. This requires us to meet people where they are in their performance. And, because no two people are ever the same, managers must be versatile in their approach and avoid one-size-fits-all formulas.

People are different, and what works for one person and generates a positive response could backfire with someone else. Far too often I hear managers describe their style and approach to leading in a one-dimensional way. This often comes across as "take-it-or-leave-it" thinking and it does not foster the kind of lateral range effective managers must possess to connect with diverse people and nurture effective performance when diverse performance gaps are present. In order to bring some structure and consistency to *how managers recognize the moments when adapting their approach is needed,* there are three categories of developmental meetings that each set the stage for what you need to accomplish based on the circumstances. The three types of meetings include:

1. The Friendly Check-In (i.e., "Let's stay on the same page while things are going well...");
2. The Concerned Check-In (i.e., "There is something I'm worried about; let's discuss before it is a big deal..."); and
3. The Problem Check-In (i.e., "We have a problem and I need you to understand why this matters...").

These examples are described below in the form of action steps for the different scenarios you will likely encounter with various reporting relationships. Working relationships are always fluid, so it is not uncommon for the Friendly Check-In to migrate to the Concerned Check-In, or for a Concerned Check-In to evolve into the Problem Check-In. The opposite is also true; a Concerned Check-In can result in the full resolution of the potential issue and ease into a more Friendly Check-In. The point is that these are not intended to label your people or box you into a strict approach; they are simply guides for you to find the right starting place with tone and approach.

Friendly Check-In (When the Supervisory Relationship Is New and/or On-Track)

I. Set up the initial conversations to:
   a. Review the standard job description and complete the Six-Question Matrix to reveal their "job-within-the-job;"
   b. Put it in Three Dimensions to identify key collaborators who will support them;
   c. Ask for the employees' input about anticipated tasks/functions that may require additional support;
   d. TELL THEM WHAT YOU EXPECT as far as ongoing communication, your management style, and preferences for completing assignments;
   e. Communicate about the specific process and performance accountabilities that are relevant to the position;
   f. Schedule weekly or biweekly check-in meetings for the first 90 days at minimum; and
   g. Document relevant agreements and expectations with objective, clear writing.

Concerned Check-In (When the Relationship Needs to Get On-Track)

I. Set up direct conversations to:
   a. Ensure that their "job-within-the-job" is clear and that no hidden challenges are directly undermining their success;
   b. Review/check the status of goals, projects, assignments, and tasks;
   c. Assess ongoing barriers and roadblocks to learning and performance goals;
   d. Anticipate and plan for any upcoming changes; and
   e. Revisit long-term professional development plans (i.e., company-sponsored events and elements from their Future-Proof plan) to tap their motivation and incentive to improve performance.

Problem Check-In (When the Relationship Is At-Risk)

I. Set up immediate conversations to:

    a. Provide clear, specific feedback to the employee regarding things they are doing well and areas requiring further improvement;

    b. Emphasize the relative importance of making the targeted improvements;

    c. Communicate directly and honestly about what is expected and the consequence of failure to deliver on those expectations;

    d. Invite the employee to share input about challenges and additional support they need;

    e. Review the most relevant, high-priority accountabilities;

    f. Give the employee assignments (e.g., you need to check back with me and demonstrate...); and

    g. Document relevant expectations and accountabilities with objective, clear writing.

HOW ARE YOU DOING WITH YOUR DIRECT REPORTS?

Beyond your active engagement and commitment to staying in regular conversation with your team members, you must also periodically take stock of your direct report status with a long-range view. This is particularly true after periods of change, adjustments in team roles and processes, or when strategic shifts require existing teams to reorient their work around a new set of objectives. You can use this two-part exercise to manage with a mind-set that continuously adjusts to the hidden side of work. Begin with the prompts in table 14.1 that reflect the management challenges you experience in the SMW, including the ways they direct you back to the hidden curriculum of work.

PART ONE

The following statements reflect successful Management Practices. Please consider and rank each item in a way that reflects where the relationship is *right now*. The goal of this exercise is to identify ways to move from left to right along the continuum in order to establish more effective, performance-based relationships with your direct reports, therefore the more accurately you rank each item, the easier it will be to plot action steps to improve them.

PART TWO

Using Part One as a guide, now look at any statements that you ranked #3 or below. These are the areas of immediate concern for you to address. For each of

Table 14.1 Ranking Effective Management Practices

Part One – Ranking Management Practices	
Direct Report: _____	Date: _____
Effective Management Practices	*Current Rank*
I establish a supportive, trust-based relationship that places the quality of the employee's working life at the center of importance.	NEVER ALWAYS 1...........2...........3...........4...........5
I accurately assess the individual's knowledge, skills, and abilities in relation to the requirements of meeting the true demands of their "job-within-the-job."	NEVER ALWAYS 1...........2...........3...........4...........5
I work with the employee to define the mutually beneficial agenda, where their vital purpose, value-added contributions, and career aspirations align with the needs of the team and the overall goals of the organization.	NEVER ALWAYS 1...........2...........3...........4...........5
I make the hidden side of work continuously discussible and invest time and resources into others' processes of refining their "job-within-the-job" as conditions change.	NEVER ALWAYS 1...........2...........3...........4...........5
I actively engage with this team member and spend time with him/her on the job.	NEVER ALWAYS 1...........2...........3...........4...........5
I have regularly scheduled 1:1 meetings with this team member and I give him/her direct feedback when needed to support his/her performance.	NEVER ALWAYS 1...........2...........3...........4...........5

Continued

Table 14.1 Continued

Part One – Ranking Management Practices	
Direct Report: _____	Date: _____
Effective Management Practices	*Current Rank*
I enjoy working with this team member and it is easy for me to supervise him/her.	NEVER ALWAYS 1...........2...........3...........4...........5
I believe this team member feels consistently engaged in his/her work.	NEVER ALWAYS 1...........2...........3...........4...........5
I ensure that this team member knows our team's top goals and is clear about his/her specific role in achieving them.	NEVER ALWAYS 1...........2...........3...........4...........5
I hold this team member accountable for doing the right things.	NEVER ALWAYS 1...........2...........3...........4...........5

Table 14.2 Action Plan

Part Two – Action Planning
Direct Report: _____
Current Status: Overall, this supervisory relationship is currently: □**Consistent & Effective** □**Okay, But Needs Improvement** □**Ineffective &At-Risk**
The two greatest challenges I currently experience with this person are: 1. _____ 2. _____
The two most important next steps I will take to improve this supervisory relationship include: 1. _____ 2. _____

your direct reports that have areas for improvement, use Table 14.2 to complete the action plan to give yourself a path forward with concrete steps.

KEY TAKEAWAYS

Once you acknowledge and fully embrace the hidden curriculum of work, you have no choice but to manage differently. Whether you have one direct report or many, there are specific ways of thinking and taking action as a manager that will facilitate the *breakthrough performance* of team members. Managing to the hidden side of work starts with the principle that *less is more* and it continues with a new definition of effective management: *helping people understand and transform the everyday challenges that prevent them from doing their best work, then getting out of the way.*

With this definition as a starting place, the commitments and practices of managers include five key drivers: (1) Establishing a supportive, trust-based relationship that balances the individual's knowledge and skills with the true demands of their job and the goals of the organization; (2) Creating expectations early and reinforcing them often; (3) Making the hidden side of work discussible and investing time and resources into others' processes of discovering their "job-within-the-job;" (4) Staying present enough to track their ongoing efforts and progress; and (5) Communicating early and often when expectations and accountabilities are unmet.

These practices lead to specific interventions that managers can apply to stay actively engaged in coordinating the roles of team members, aligning work flows with organizational priorities, and simultaneously creating a culture that reflects the demands of the hidden side of work and the support of individuals to overcome its challenges. The two-part assessment allows you to take stock of where you are right now with your direct reports, including the specific steps you can follow to engage with them to improve performance initially and over time.

Chapter 15

CULTIVATING FUTURE-PROOF LEADERS AND ORGANIZATIONAL CULTURES

THE SENSE OF PERSONAL EMPOWERMENT and measurable performance improvement that comes along with successfully navigating your own hidden curriculum of work can help you thrive. If you want your team and the greater organization to gain the related motivation and capacity, then you must also look at the navigation tools of *Beyond the Job Description* as a *leadership* and *culture change* endeavor, not just as a set of tools for personal and professional development.

The last phase of the R-I-T-E Model – Establishing a culture of continuous learning and performance – requires a discussion about **both** organizational culture and leadership. This is because leaders play such a pivotal role in the process of creating and changing organizational culture that you cannot discuss culture change without acknowledging the fundamental role and impact of leaders. The purpose of this chapter is to offer specific strategies and related action steps to cultivate effective leaders who can make the cultural changes in your organization required to effectively respond to the hidden curriculum of work. Although distinct books could be written about both themes separately, I will summarize the key points and essential take-aways here, beginning with organization culture.[1]

A NEW DEFINITION OF ORGANIZATIONAL CULTURE

Do we really need another definition of organization culture? It is true that organization culture has many descriptions; however, considering the implications of *Beyond the Job Description,* a legitimate update is needed. In general terms, culture can be defined as the learned, shared, and transmitted behaviors among members of an organization. The way people within organizations interpret their experience and assign meaning to the actions they take also reflects culture. I personally like this straightforward definition of culture: *it is just the way things get done around here.*[2]

While this is a short, sweet, and deceptively profound description, it still misses a fundamental point. *Beyond the Job Description* requires a definition that accounts for the fluid and creative ways that things get done in organizations, but also what those patterns and connections *make.* Therefore, I define organizational culture as *the ecosystem of patterns of communication and interaction.*

This "ecosystem of patterns"—from everyday hallway conversations, staff meetings, and policy updates, to major strategy decisions—directly influences the quality of working life for people inside the organization and it influences their level of (1) engagement; (2) learning; (3) performance; and (4) overall contribution.

Sustaining high levels of these four factors can lead to bottom-line success for the organization and the virtuous cycle that follows: healthy relationships among engaged people, doing their best work, in a profitable company, which produces healthier, more engaged people doing even better work as they contribute increasingly to the long-term success of the organization.

When people join an organization they go through a process of assimilation where they absorb the rules and norms of their new culture. This begins with the very first set of interactions during the recruitment and selection process, and it accelerates during the first few weeks of employment. In this process people learn what members of a culture think, do, and say and it helps people make sense of their experience in the organization.[3] While they are in the process of absorbing and assimilating, they also begin to co-influence these same learned, shared, and transmitted elements of the culture. It follows that if organization culture is made in the small, day-to-day interactions among people, then any culture change must also begin with shifts in these everyday patterns of interaction.

ORGANIZATIONS ARE MADE, NOT FOUND

Now that we have a working definition of organizational culture, we can step back and look at the nature of organizations themselves. The intrinsic nature of our organizational lives was summed up perfectly by the sociologist Amitai Etzioni when he said:

> Our society is an organizational society. We are born in organizations, educated in organizations, and most of us spend much of our lives working for organizations. We spend much of our leisure time playing and praying in organizations. Most of us will die in an organization, and when the time comes for burial, the largest organization of all—the state—must grant official permission.[4]

The way in which we live out our lives embedded in organizations can lead to a faulty assumption that organizations exist, as they are, and we simply find them and join them. On the contrary: *organizations are made, not found.*

> To facilitate lasting culture change, leaders must be intentional about what they talk about, how they talk about it, and the extent to which their actions are consistent with what they say. When the hidden curriculum of work is at the center of the conversation, going *beyond the job description* and achieving *breakthrough performance* becomes a cultural expectation.

So, how are organizations made? An organization is made through the ongoing and combined actions of its people. This simple idea brings us back to our new definition of culture. The intricate system of ongoing patterns of communication and interaction create culture, and organizations are, in effect, reflections of the culture its members create and sustain. When you consider that the basis for any action is communication, another way of expressing this is that "communication . . . is the very essence of a social system or organization."[5]

PEOPLE STAY OR GO BECAUSE OF THIS STUFF

People do not leave organizations to seek out other opportunities because of communication, leadership, or culture. They leave because of what communication, leadership, and culture *make* or *do not make* in their experience at work. The primary lens through which most people seem to evaluate their ability to remain in a job with their organization is the quality of their direct relationship with their supervisor. If the patterns are productive and reasonably conducive to a satisfactory working life, then people typically stay. When they get past the point of tolerable, people who have a choice will often leave that organization.

Moving beyond the fundamental supervisor-employee relationship, another prominent area that people evaluate is the character and impact of the organization's culture. In other words, what do those ongoing patterns of communication and interaction produce in their everyday experiences? Are these outcomes consistent with their values? Do they bring out the best in them, or do they foster qualities that do not match their expectations for how work gets done and people are treated? In exit interviews—those final conversations between an employee who is leaving an organization and the human resources department—a new level of truth telling often occurs. With the mind-set of "what can they really do to me, I've already quit!" people often provide honest assessments about communication, leadership, and culture including the real reasons for the resignations. When they are candid people may say things like:

- "I don't agree with how things are done here, the culture of this organization doesn't match my values."
- I don't feel supported here; I'm asked to do the job of three people and that just isn't sustainable."
- "I love our mission and the people that I work with...but the way decisions are made and the amount of procedural 'stuff' we have to go through is just too much."
- "It doesn't seem like the left-hand knows what the right-hand is doing. There is just no effective communication about the big picture."
- "I don't feel like I can trust people here and so I need to move on to a healthier place to work."
- "The culture here is just too toxic; I can't stay here any longer."

While some of these statements may seem extreme, I have heard them many times in my experience as a manager and human resources executive. When it really comes down to it, this vast thing that we call *culture* is just a reflection of the stories we tell about our experience on the job. Too often these experiences and challenges are described using the language of "them" vs. "us." Any realistic effort to change a culture requires the dissolution of the line between "us" and "them." As individuals, we are the culture of our organizations. One of the fundamental mandates of a leader is to help people on their teams to embrace the fact that they are partners in the process of creating and sustaining culture.

And, if we want better organizations and organizational cultures that create the conditions where the *mutual agenda* can be achieved, then we have to make them by first changing our own experience.

CULTURE EVOLVES AT THREE LEVELS

Using this expanded definition of organization culture as a foundation, we can return to the last stage of the R-I-T-E Model. This final phase is intended to solidify the deeper shifts that occurred throughout the prior steps in the process and to further extend those within the organization. Lasting culture change requires the engagement of all three levels of the organization—individual, team, and the overall organization. Activating reflexive loops at all three levels extends the cycle of continuous learning and performance in this way:

- Individuals—Individuals are given context by leaders about the market conditions, business challenges/opportunities, and clear strategic priorities. Individuals are empowered to explore their "job-within-the-job" and they commit to and practice transforming barriers into opportunities for learning and performance, which connects their own goals back to the greater team and organizational objectives.
- Teams—Teams are trusted by leaders to enact change as needed to effectively respond to evolving conditions that affect the organization. The individual members of the team are accountable for prioritizing learning and performance in relation to the overall priorities of the team, as well as for using Nav-Maps to resolve issues as they surface.
- Organizations—Organizations maintain the structure (i.e., policies, procedures, resource allocations, and written/unwritten rules, etc.) that releases the passion, commitment, and full engagement of individuals and teams. Organizations provide information, context, and ongoing capacity to support pursuits that get their people Future-Proofed and direct their highest contributions to the mutual agenda.

When there is activity at each of these three levels, cultures can go from being dominated by the SMW to embracing the true challenges of the hidden side of work. With this background and understanding of organizational culture, we can now focus on the specific role that leaders play in the culture change process.

A NEW DEFINITION OF LEADERSHIP

Whether we consciously choose to or not, we make the ongoing patterns of communication and interaction (i.e., organization culture) that shape the experiences and outcomes we have throughout our working lives. Collectively, these patterns reflect the character of our teams and give the culture of our organization its identity. Although every member of the organization contributes, leaders have extreme influence over the specific patterns that influence culture because of their presumed knowledge, skill, and ability, as well as through their active engagement in overlapping contexts (i.e., decision-making meetings, reporting relationships, agenda-setting venues, etc.) where action is taken on the priorities that matter most. By virtue of their cross-cutting function, leaders are pivotal players in many of the central patterns that make organizations.

> Leaders are *the chief architects of the patterns of communication and interaction that make organization culture.*

In this new definition, leaders play a critical role in fostering talent and making the most productive use of it. Leaders enable discussion, champion follow-through, reward people for doing what makes a difference, and hold others accountable when they underperform. The authority and resources to do these things well put them in a unique seat of influence for inspiring and leading teams beyond the job description. While the collective efforts of every person in the organization contribute to the ongoing patterns that ultimately shape the culture and performance of the company, leaders play a significant role in influencing the day-to-day experience of staff, which in turn creates and sustains the major elements of low- and high-performing organizational cultures.

Seeing the hidden side of work provides leaders with the opportunity to bring greater focused attention to critical elements in their organization. The practices introduced throughout this book have already offered a scaled approach to seeing the world of work from various vantage points. Seeing your "job-within-the-job" is like the 15,000 ft. view. Navigating the hidden challenges of work is like the 1,000 ft. view. And proactively delivering your vital purpose, value-added contributions, and turning barriers into opportunities for improved learning and performance everyday is being at ground-level in real-time. These mixed-level vantage points can help leaders bring the hidden side of work into the critical conversations of organizational change, including the following day-to-day objectives:

1. *Scan the SMW for signs of the Hidden Curriculum of Work*
   a. Change frames from the SMW to the hidden curriculum of work to alter the way you process and understand the world of work;
   b. Continuously observe what happens within the organization and watch out for the moments when the important work to be done is potentially undermined by the hidden side of work;
   c. Focus on a clear picture of what matters, including your own vital purpose, value-added contributions, and challenges from the "job-within-the-job;"
   d. Use a common language to name the true challenges of work; and
   e. Create a culture of expectations, accountability, and support for team members to examine their "job-within-the-job" and to navigate its challenges.

2. *Select Patterns of Interaction from the SMW That Undermine Success*
   a. Identify the old habits of work and patterns of interaction that undermine the most important priorities and true demands of work;
   b. Use the practice of making Nav-Maps to address specific barriers and challenges in real-time; and
   c. Reorient the organizational structure (i.e., recruit and hire based on the hidden curriculum of work and design policies, procedures, resource allocations accordingly) around the needs of the hidden curriculum of work.

3. *Commit Time, Energy, and Resources to the Growth of Future Leaders*
   a. Engage others to reveal the hidden curriculum of work; and
   b. Turn followers into leaders by empowering them to actively contribute to the necessary changes to meet its demands.

As leaders go through these three cycles, they gain confidence in the practice of seeing the ecosystem of their team's work, including specific ways to make the hidden curriculum of work discussable and the primary focus of the way things get done. Perhaps the most advantageous upside for leaders to see the hidden curriculum of work and advocate for the same approach with their teams is that it can help them meet three of the most common challenges and opportunities facing today's leaders:

- **Accomplishing More with Less:** No organization is immune to the inverse relationship of shrinking resources and growing expectations. In the face of continuing competition and resource limitations, individuals and teams are increasingly being asked to accomplish more with less. Positioning active, high-performing leaders to navigate the hidden curriculum of work can help organizations to maximize the resources reflected in their human capital, making it easier to solve the equation of *doing more with less.*

- **The Multiplication of Benefits with the Integration of New Skills:** As leaders exercise their navigation competencies and related skills, those abilities naturally tend to proliferate across the organization. Leaders that dive into the hidden curriculum of work and successfully improve the most challenging patterns will inspire others to do the same. As this informal transfer of knowledge/skill influences others throughout the organization, the benefits of greater capacity and improved team performance multiply as well.

- **Increased Positive Conflict and Greater Team Cohesion:** The costs of negative, unresolved conflict represent one of the most reducible business costs on a balance sheet. However, productive conflict that results in increased creativity and greater team cohesion after positive resolution offers a catalyst for change. Leaders that navigate the hidden curriculum of work by definition often produce creative dissent (i.e., productive disagreement that results in better decisions, planning, and overall responses to opportunities) because of the way in which they push past limited expectations. Because these areas of divergence are substantive, not personality driven, these are often inspiring challenges and they can be framed as a source of positive conflict and a pathway toward greater team cohesion.

EVIDENCE OF A "BREAKTHROUGH CULTURE"

If you wonder precisely what it would look like, sound like, and feel like if your team and organization adopted the principles and practices of *Beyond the Job Description,* the following summary provides a glimpse of that transformation.

I developed this list of the major elements of breakthrough cultures by observing the experience of my clients and by studying the effects of people who navigate their hidden curriculum of work. In some ways, this set of standards draws on familiar themes, including elements of the Great Place to Work Culture audit model:[6]

Individuals will say, think, and feel...

- I feel supported in my efforts to get my best work done and to succeed in my role;
- I have the necessary resources to do my job effectively;
- I receive recognition for a job well done;
- I have opportunities to learn and advance in my career; and
- I receive competitive compensation and opportunities to grow.

Teams will interact in ways that reflect...

- People understand and respect each others' hidden challenges of work;
- People work hard to get the job done;
- People are trusted to contribute and perform well;
- People are informed about potential changes and important issues when they surface; and
- People look forward to coming to work and there is a sense of purpose beyond just "having a job."

Organizational leaders will...

- Understand the true experience of people, including accurate assessments of their workloads and demands of the job;
- Encourage mistakes through trial and error because innovation is important;
- Be approachable and provide venues for honest conversation about real challenges;
- Be open to feedback and suggestions for improvement; and
- Focus on effective results and avoid playing favorites with people.

These factors reflect the potential of *Beyond the Job Description* to result in lasting culture change. Going from increases in individual performance, to enhanced team effectiveness, the virtuous cycle that can be established when the hidden curriculum of work is made visible, discussible, and navigable is powerful.

OVERCOMING THE FIRST BARRIER TO CULTURE CHANGE

While leaders may encounter a variety of obstacles to achieving lasting culture change, there is one fundamental challenge that requires immediate focused attention. It has to do with habits that many people adopt, which produce a rigid resistance to change.

Early in life we learn ways to compensate for the risks and threats we perceive by developing patterns of behavior that help us avoid them. Despite the fact that these avoidance behaviors often do not adhere to common sense, we tend to repeat them over time. For example, if we are afraid of being seen as incompetent, we might avoid asking questions that potentially reveal our lack of knowledge. The predictable impact is that by avoiding asking questions, we fail to acquire the information we need, which further sustains the ongoing gap in knowledge.

The seminal Harvard academic and pioneer of organizational learning theory and practice, Chris Argyris, referred to these patterns of behavior as *defensive routines*.[7] By their very nature, defensive routines are self-maintaining and self-reinforcing, which prevents learning and correction. Despite the blind spots they often create—whether they include avoidance, scapegoating, or other forms of diversion—we maintain them because we believe that they will help us evade challenging, threatening, or otherwise embarrassing problems. Because these habits of thinking and action are formed early, they become part of our standard way of operating.

In the same way that individuals adopt defensive routines, teams and organizations do so as well. For example, the *Mum Effect*—a term coined by social science researchers Sydney Rosen and Abraham Tesser—is a defensive routine where people avoid sharing undesirable information for fear of being associated with it.[8] In other words, people sometimes avoid the facts and withhold information (even if it could be valuable to understand and take action on) to avoid potentially challenging or threatening reactions. Overemphasizing past success and underemphasizing potential competitive threats are other tendencies, or defensive routines, that teams and organizations often follow.

In the same way there is also a systemic, defensive routine embedded in the SMW. This shows up in the form of avoidance of the true demands of work and a structural lack of accountability for establishing the *mutual agenda* and consistently meeting the challenges of the hidden curriculum of work.

If you are an employee, what could be more threatening than to acknowledge that you do not know what your true job is or how to successfully meet its challenges? If you are a manager, what could be more embarrassing than acknowledging that you do not know what is required for your direct reports to fully deliver their greatest contributions to the team in order to deliver results for the organization? And, when the organization's culture insulates people from these kinds of honest, performance-driven conversations, what could be more devastating to a career than being the only one to step forward and admit to these gaps?

As a result of this defensive routine, people in organizations become highly skilled at maintaining the SMW because it avoids an honest assessment of the obstacles and threats that the true challenges of work present. For individuals and leaders, uncovering your hidden path to success at work requires you to identify the various self-maintaining, self-reinforcing, antilearning, and noncorrective features that sustain the defensive routines.

One could argue with the central premise in this book by saying, *"Workers around the world could not possibly be so blind that the true nature of work is hidden from them in plain sight!"* My response to this is that people at work are actually not "blind" to this. They are fully aware of the presence of challenges; they simply do not have a language to identify and name them, nor do they have accessible frameworks to address them. Instead, people are left to figure it out on their own.

Some try and are successful (but not without heavy investments in time and energy and the scars to show for it), others try and fail, but most just ignore it through defensive routines that delay the inevitable confrontation with work's true demands. Organizations are simply a reflection of the cumulative patterns of behavior of their people, so this ongoing avoidance "protects individual from becoming aware of these conditions and from accepting responsibility for creating and maintaining them."[9]

LEADERS ARE THE SCAFFOLDING FOR OTHERS TO CLIMB

With the understanding that the SMW's core defensive routine must be addressed first, here are seven final suggestions that bring the concepts of leadership and culture change together in a game plan leaders can execute to jump-start the culture change process:

1. One of the most important things you can do for others is to give them a leg up at work. Putting your reputation and influence behind a rising star, sticking with someone who maintains a contentious perspective when it is needed, and investing your time and energy to help someone else grow are just three examples of *sponsoring* someone at work.

2. As a leader, when you sponsor another person's growth and development, you provide them with the scaffolding to reach new heights that they would otherwise not have access to. One of the most powerful ways to sponsor someone for long-term success is to support them in the process of discovering their "job-within-the-job" and revealing their hidden curriculum of work. It could be said that a leader's vital purpose is to help others to discover their own.

3. Wherever you are on the organization chart, make lots of Nav-Maps, demonstrate their effectiveness, socialize them internally, and connect their positive effects to business outcomes.

4. Nav-Maps teach people indirectly about the significance of root cause problem solving and taking a systemic perspective. The more that you invite others into the process of making Nav-Maps, especially those who may be resistant, the more you extend these important organizational success factors.

5. When making Nav-Maps, take steps to simplify the four stages as needed to model the principles, rather than the process (Meaning: if you only have ten minutes with a reluctant team member, just make a constellation. Don't feel like you have to do the whole process at once.).

6. Make themes like "The Mutual Agenda," and "Future-Proof Teams" relevant to senior managers within the organization by showing them the bottom-line truth. Emphasize the cycle of individual performance within the effects of team and organizational outcomes.

7. Integrate the concepts of navigating the hidden curriculum and getting Future-Proofed into your organization's reward/incentive program for current employees, as well as your recruitment and selection process for new employees. By "putting your money where your mouth is," you go beyond a casual buy-in of this alterative view of work and give people reason to go along on the journey.

BENEFITS OF IMPLEMENTING "BEYOND THE JOB DESCRIPTION PRACTICES"

To conclude this chapter I will highlight two final benefits that senior leaders can expect when they implement the concepts and practices of *Beyond the Job Description*. The first major benefit of adopting these practices in the workplace is that it enlists executive leaders, senior managers, and line-level supervisors in a systematic, straightforward approach to identifying and closing performance gaps. Because the kinds of interpersonal, behavioral gaps are often the hardest to close due to their complex human elements, the system adds value by providing a concrete language and objective set of criteria to close the gaps and address related concerns.

When implemented, one of the most significant impacts of the system is that it broadly inspires a culture of learning and performance. Rather than internal competition that reduces effective collaboration, *Beyond the Job Description* does not frame continuous learning and performance as a zero-sum game where there are winners and losers. Cultivating more top performers can make individuals better, and it also makes teams and organizations thrive.

The second major benefit is that with time constraints and levels of responsibility that often make it difficult for leaders to talk to employees, the system provides a common way of connecting the organization via the *mutual agenda*. The mutual agenda is the alignment between individual goals for high performance and success, and related team and organizational priorities. For example, when an executive leader asks employees about their hidden challenges of work, employees are acknowledged and validated according to the real-world obstacles they face. And, they can have meaningful exchanges about needs, resources, and support that will improve their performance. Likewise, leaders receive more candid assessments of issues and concern that impact performance and affect the bottom line. This avoids the very common defensive routine that occurs during sporadic communication with leaders/ employees whereby people withhold bad news for fear of being associated with it.

KEY TAKEAWAYS

The last phase of the R-I-T-E Model is about establishing a culture of continuous learning and performance. Because leaders play such a pivotal role in the process of creating and changing organizational culture, you cannot discuss culture change without acknowledging the role leaders play in the process.

Beyond the Job Description requires a definition that accounts not only for the fluid and creative way things get done in organizations, but also what those patterns of communication *make*. Culture is *the ecosystem of our patterns of communication and interaction*. And, organizational leaders are the *lead architects of the patterns of communication and interaction that take place in organizations*. While it is the collective effort of every person in the organization to contribute to the patterns that ultimately shape the culture and performance of the company, leaders play a significant role in influencing the day-to-day experience of staff, which in turn creates and sustains many of the major elements of organizational culture.

Thinking about organizations as an ecosystem of patterns that directly influence the quality of working life for people inside the organization has implications on levels of engagement, learning, performance, and overall contribution. Sustaining high levels of these four factors can lead to bottom-line success for the organization and the virtuous cycle that follows: healthy relationships among engaged people, doing their best work, in a profitable company, which produces healthier, more engaged people doing even better work as they contribute increasingly to the long-term success of the organization. There are specific strategies and related action steps that you can take to cultivate effective leaders who can make the cultural changes in your organization required to effectively respond to the hidden challenges of work. Seven things that leaders can do to *be the scaffolding for others to climb* include initiatives that range from sponsoring others, to leading Nav-Map making sessions.

Appendix 1

SELF-ASSESSMENT: HOW FUTURE-PROOF ARE YOU?

THE PURPOSE OF THIS SELF-ASSESSMENT is to help you identify your current response pattern to the everyday challenges you face at work. For most people, their orientation toward work is based on the Standard Model of Work (SMW), which follows a superficial interpretation of the definition of success on the job. This approach fails to recognize the importance of understanding your "job-within-the-job," and the myriad challenges from the hidden curriculum of work that reduce learning and performance and erode the quality of your working life.

INSTRUCTIONS

Read each statement below and consider each of the three possible responses. Circle the response that most closely matches your preference. While you may or may not have experienced similar scenarios directly, imagine that you are personally facing the circumstance and choose the response and course of action that you would most likely take. Once you answer all of the questions, add the total numerical score and record your number in the *Total Box* below. To interpret your score, find the corresponding range that matches your number in the *Profile Descriptions* at the conclusion of the assessment.

SELF-ASSESSMENT QUESTIONS

QUESTION ONE

It is 9:15 am and you are just getting into the rhythm of your day. Your phone rings, and on the other end of the line one of your colleagues unexpectedly asks you to attend a meeting that starts in just 45 minutes. Although you respect this colleague and ideally would like to support her, you had plans for your morning and are getting closer to a few deadlines with your own priorities. How would you respond to the meeting invitation?

1. Stick to my existing plan and graciously say "no."
2. Let my colleague know that I will attend the meeting and offer input if I can, but clearly set a boundary that I will not be able stay longer than one hour because of my own priorities and timelines.
3. Ask a few questions about the anticipated goals and importance of the meeting. Then, quickly evaluate whether my vital purpose and value-added contributions could positively impact the outcome of the meeting and make a decision based on that.

QUESTION TWO

You have just returned to your desk after another frustrating interaction with a colleague. Rather than communicating clearly about the project, it seems like you keep butting heads and getting in each other's way. As you mentally review what just happened and try to decompress from the difficult conversation, you conclude that:

1. You and your colleague will just not get along, so it is best to try to work around them.
2. Collaboration is an important factor in team success, so you will just have to keep trying to get through to them, no matter what it takes.
3. You focus your attention on where the specific breakdown in communication shows up. Using tools to understand the problem, you make an effort to get to the root cause of the issue so that the frustrating experience does not escalate or diminish your performance.

QUESTION THREE

Your annual review comes up and your boss has asked you to complete a self-assessment in advance of your performance evaluation. She has given you a copy of your job description and asked you to indicate "successes" and "challenges" from the last year. As you complete the self-assessment portion, you write down:

1. The list of last year's "successes" and "challenges" that correspond to your primary tasks and activities.

2. The list of last year's "successes" and "challenges" that correspond to your tasks and activities, as well as requests for support in areas that you would like to grow.

3. A statement that summarizes your overall effort to deliver your vital purpose and value-added contributions over the last year, including specific examples (both reflected in the job description and beyond the job description) of your impacts on the team through those efforts. In addition, you draft a list of the ongoing challenges that prevent your best work, including suggested action steps you would like to pursue with your manager's support.

QUESTION FOUR

You are accountable for responding to potential customers via e-mail who have downloaded a free information guide on your company's website. When you were trained to do this follow-up, you were given specific expectations and scripts to use. For the last three months you have faithfully completed the task according to these guidelines; however, you recently noticed that the outcomes of your efforts have been inconsistent. Recognizing that the inconsistency is due to a lack of customization, you conclude that there is a more effective way to respond to these potential customers. You decide to:

1. Wait and see if your manager asks for input.
2. Look for an opening to proactively bring up the idea at a future staff meeting.
3. Take initiative to understand and describe the precise opportunity, including the steps that would be necessary to implement the change. You mock up a sample of the alternative response using an actual case in order to demonstrate the potential effectiveness of the innovative approach. Then, you schedule a meeting with the decision makers to gather their input and get potential buy-in for the change.

QUESTION FIVE

You have been "stuck in a rut" for the last six months and are starting to consider a job change. You like your company, but lately you have been feeling underchallenged and undervalued for your potential. You decide to:

1. Immediately start putting feelers out.

2. Share your thoughts with your manager to see if they can address your concerns.

3. Consider the options of starting a job search and speaking with your manager, but start with an exploration of your hidden curriculum of work. Knowing that you are the single most significant influence on the quality of your working life, you honestly assess gaps between your purpose and contributions and your everyday experience. You also look for hidden challenges that may be eroding your motivation to stay engaged. If this evaluation confirms that you are not in a place to get back on track and ultimately achieve the working life you want, you then exercise your other options with a clear reason for the change.

QUESTION SIX

You have worked at your company for two years. Initially, one of your favorite things about working there was the fact that people were professional and polite to one another. Over time, however, you have come to realize that what you once considered "politeness" is actually an avoidance of important issues and concerns. You are not a vocal person, nor are you a formal leader in the company. Considering these facts, you decide to:

1. Live with the situation and hope that it will change in the future.

2. Decide to go out of your comfort zone and speak up the next time you feel strongly about an issue.

3. Recognize that great work cannot be accomplished without open communication, and then seek an opportunity to discuss ways to facilitate better exchanges of viewpoints with open-minded leaders. And, without making things personal, draw the pattern of interaction that prevents effective communication in order to highlight its damaging impacts on information sharing, decision making, and trust building.

QUESTION SEVEN

The senior vice president of your division announces a major strategy change at an all-hands staff meeting. The change is a big surprise to most people, and the related shift in priorities likely means that several of the projects you have been working on will be overhauled or abandoned. Your initial reaction to the announcement is:

1. Frustration from being blindsided by the change.
2. Uncertainty about the future, but you make an effort to roll with the change.
3. Understanding that continuous change is hard, but inevitable, and that these unexpected shifts are sometimes out of your control. Then, assessing the specific implications of the announcement on your workload, you look for specific ways to contribute to the goals of the new strategy while preparing to advocate for what you believe is important to continue.

QUESTION EIGHT

Your organization has faced a series of steep financial hurdles, and the CEO just announced a hiring freeze, wage freeze, and cut to the health benefits that employees receive. After hearing this news, you decide to:

1. Coast in your duties because you feel that you are being treated unfairly.
2. Seriously consider your future with the company, including whether you can stay in light of the recent cutbacks.
3. Recognize that now, more than ever, the organization requires outstanding performance from all team members. Spend time assessing the vital purpose and value-added contributions that you can make to ensure that the organization is getting your best. Make an effort to work with others to identify and resolve hidden challenges that may be preventing consistent and effective performance across the organization. And, in addition to these efforts, assess your career goals and the impact of these cutbacks on the quality of your working life to honestly evaluate your future at the organization.

SCORING THE ASSESSMENT

In the box below, write your total score by counting up the numerical value of your combined responses. For example if you circled #2 in all eight of the questions, your total score would be 16.

Total Score: _____		
A total score of 8–12 *"Sinking in the SMW"*	A total score of 13–16 *"Treading Water in the HCW"*	A total score of 17–24 *"Navigating the HCW"*

HOW FUTURE-PROOF ARE YOU?: PROFILE DESCRIPTIONS

Your capacity to shift from the SMW and recognize your hidden curriculum of work is reflected in your responses to this self-assessment exercise. The following interpretation of your score provides a starting place for action. While these are general descriptions, they do include specific recommendations for next steps that you can take to more effectively respond to the true demands of your work.

- A score of 8–12 = *Sinking in the SMW*
  - ○ *Sinking means that you are overmatched by the hidden side of work, which keeps you in constant "catch-up mode" and feeling like you are literally "going under water" or near the point of burnout.*
  - ○ If you are in this state of crisis, take immediate action with the following steps:
    1. Complete the Six-Question Matrix to identify your "job-within-the-job;"
    2. Take the BLPA to identify the barriers to learning and performance that prevent your best work;
    3. Make Nav-Maps for the top two barriers in order to develop positive, forward-looking action plans that will empower you to get ahead of the daily demands of your work; and
    4. Following this concentrated effort, make your Future-Proof Plan to create a clearer vision about the fundamental changes you want to make to get your career on the trajectory you want.

- A score of 13–16 = *Treading Water in the HCW*
  - ○ *Treading Water means you are consistently overmatched by the hidden side of work, which requires a continuous struggle to keep enough resources and energy available to prevent sinking. At certain times you may feel like you catch your breath and start to move forward, but these bursts are short-lived, and when the next wave of challenges arrives you lack the stamina and direction to keep your eyes on the horizon.*
  - ○ If you are in this state of potential risk, take immediate action with the following steps:
    1. Complete the Six-Question Matrix to identify your "job-within-the-job;"

2. Take the BLPA to identify the barriers to learning and performance that prevent your best work;

3. Make Nav-Maps for the top two barriers in order to develop positive, forward-looking action plans that will empower you to get ahead of the daily demands of your work; and

4. Following this concentrated effort, make your Future-Proof Plan to create a clearer vision about the fundamental changes you want to make to get your career on the trajectory you want.

- A score of 17–24 = *Navigating the HCW*
  - o *Navigating means you see and are actively engaged in meeting the hidden curriculum of work. You may still have some bad days, but overall you are aware of your vital purpose and are able to deliver your value-added contributions amidst the changing demands of your work. Being in tune with the hidden curriculum of work, including the real-time challenges and opportunities that it brings your way, enables you to actively shape the quality of your working life. You are on your path to getting Future-Proofed!*
  - o If you are in this state of positive movement, take immediate action with the following steps:
    1. Refine your Six-Question Matrix to affirm your "job-within-the-job" and create additional challenges for yourself to contribute a more diverse range of value-added contributions;
    2. Scan your world of work for the most subtle challenges (that have eluded you to this point) and make Nav-Maps for these barriers to develop positive, forward-looking action plans that empower you to get ahead of the daily demands of your work;
    3. Fine-tune your Future-Proof Plan to stay on your positive climb and to seek ways to accelerate the progress that will move you toward your goals; and
    4. Look for opportunities to give someone else a leg up and teach them how to more effectively see and navigate their hidden curriculum of work.

If you are "Sinking" or "Treading Water," do not worry. To uncover your hidden path to success at work you will need to understand and practice the tools of *Beyond the Job Description*. Once you gain confidence applying these tools you will be able to identify and transform barriers into opportunities for improved learning and performance and make intentional adjustments in your attitude, knowledge, skills, and abilities to stay ahead of the change curve and remain relevant at work.

Appendix 2

THE 40-STATEMENT BLPA

THE BARRIERS TO LEARNING AND Performance Assessment (BLPA) is a high-throughput instrument that enables comparative exploration and parallel analysis of barriers to learning and performance experienced by individuals and teams. The BLPA consists of a series of statements that reflect the most commonly experienced barriers to workplace learning and performance that often go unidentified within the hidden curriculum of work. The instrument was validated through rigorous research and practice.

The 10-question short version was included in chapter 6 and the full 40-question BLPA is included here. Overall, the tool can be used to assist individuals and teams to: (A) Engage stakeholders in a constructive process to explore issues of concern; (B) Integrate a diversity of viewpoints across various levels of the organization; (C) Identify and validate factors that are the causes of learning and performance gaps; (D) Reveal complex interrelationships and unexpected connections between people and issues; (E) Create deeper knowledge and awareness of isolated and shared experiences in the workplace; and (F) Leverage the specific identification of barriers to workplace learning and performance to design solutions.

Specifically, the BLPA is intended for individual users, professional development support personnel (i.e., human resources professionals, consultants, coaches, etc.), and managers who require workplace learning and performance tools to increase the performance of their teams. The administration of the assessment can be completed by, among others:

- Individuals who are required to identify and resolve their ongoing challenges with learning and performance in order to stand out and stay ahead of the change curve;

- Emerging and established managers who are responsible for managing people and utilizing the human capital within their teams for continuously improving results;

- Human resource professionals and training and development specialists within organizations who provide their constituents with easy-to-use tools for professional development, leadership growth, and team effectiveness; and

- Internally facing and externally facing consultants (organization development, facilitators, coaches, mediators, etc.) who invest in knowledge, practical tools, and professional development resources that they can immediately apply with their clients in the pursuit of improved learning and performance.

THE STATEMENTS

The BLPA is made up of 40 statements that were refined through research and practice.[1] The statements are based on the sequential and mutually reinforcing relationships identified among seven interrelated dimensions of barriers. More than simple categories, each of the seven dimensions was carefully developed through a Q-Method study that used factor analysis to discern the most common and high-impact barriers experienced in the workplace. The framework is presented in Figure A2.1. Within the image, the relationships and influences

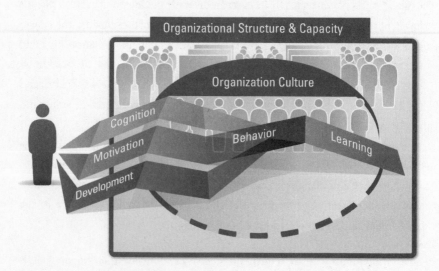

Figure A2.1   Framework of Barriers to Learning and Performance

among each of the seven dimensions are indicated by the specific orientation and placement of each component.

While it is not essential that the category of each barrier is identified, it can be useful to understand the interrelationships between barriers and their corresponding dimension. The BLPA allows the user to rank the frequency and impact of their experience with the 40 sample barriers that reflect the combination of these seven dimensions. Each dimension is abbreviated based on its corresponding acronym (i.e., Organization Culture barriers are referenced as "OC," Behavior barriers are "B," Learning barriers are "L," Cognition barriers are "C," Motivation barriers are "M," Organizational Structure and Capacity barriers are "OSC," and Development barriers are "D.").

BLPA INSTRUCTIONS

Thank you for agreeing to complete this brief assessment. It will take approximately 15–20 minutes to complete. Please read each statement and then rank it according to "frequency" and "impact" with a 1, 2, 3 or 4, depending upon how often you observe the specific barrier during your experience in the workplace and how impactful it is when experienced.

SCORING THE ASSESSMENT

To score the assessment, identify the barriers that have a combined score of between six and eight. A score of six, seven, or eight reflects a barrier that is "often" or "frequently" experienced, and when it is experienced, the impact is "obvious and challenging" or "unavoidable and destructive." Using the scoring box below, transfer the names of each barrier into the corresponding dimension. Once the assessment is completed and scored, you have a set of data points to create a "map" of your barriers as seen in Figure Appendix 2.2

DIMENSIONS OF BARRIERS

Total Rank:	OC	B	L	M	C	OSC	D

Although the specific barriers may seem convoluted and largely unrelated at first, plotting them within the framework of barriers establishes a dynamic

Table A2.1 The 40-Statement BLPA

Frequency Ratings	Impact Ratings
1 = I *Rarely* experience this barrier in the workplace.	1 = When I experience this barrier the impact is ***insignificant and negligible.***
2 = I *Sometimes* experience this barrier in the workplace.	2 = When I experience this barrier the impact is noticeable and bothersome.
3 = I *Often* experience this barrier in the workplace.	3 = When I experience this barrier the impact is obvious and challenging.
4 = I *Frequently* experience this barrier in the workplace.	4 = When I experience this barrier the impact is unavoidable and destructive.

Description of Learning & Performance Barriers	Frequency	Impact	(Mapping)
1. Absence of dialogue and limited expression of diverse viewpoints	1 2 3 4	1 2 3 4	OC
2. Accomplishing lesser priorities well while failing to focus on top goals	1 2 3 4	1 2 3 4	B
3. Lack of reflection and learning from past successes and failures	1 2 3 4	1 2 3 4	D
4. Adopting novel, popular learning solutions that do not address relevant needs	1 2 3 4	1 2 3 4	L
5. An organizational culture in which individuals experience fear and distrust	1 2 3 4	1 2 3 4	OC
6. Inability/unwillingness to adapt to fast-changing, complex, or uncertain conditions	1 2 3 4	1 2 3 4	OSC
7. Anxiety, distraction, or avoidance due to communication and information overload	1 2 3 4	1 2 3 4	M
8. Attempting to implement new behaviors without changing the old system	1 2 3 4	1 2 3 4	B
9. Attributing successes to one's own abilities/efforts while blaming failures on others	1 2 3 4	1 2 3 4	C
10. Addressing only superficial issues without solving root causes problems	1 2 3 4	1 2 3 4	L
11. An organizational culture that enables polarized views and split alliances	1 2 3 4	1 2 3 4	OC

Continued

Table A2.1 Continued

Description of Learning & Performance Barriers	Frequency	Impact	(Mapping)
12. Competitive culture that promotes individual winners, not team success	1 2 3 4	1 2 3 4	OC
13. Covert/overt bullying, threatening, and sabotaging behaviors	1 2 3 4	1 2 3 4	B
14. Deflecting criticism, scapegoating, and blaming others without accountability	1 2 3 4	1 2 3 4	B
15. Emotional, confrontational, reactive, or personality-driven patterns of behavior	1 2 3 4	1 2 3 4	B
16. Failing to change due to a victim mentality or belief that things should be different	1 2 3 4	1 2 3 4	C
17. Failing to relate new ideas and learning outcomes to on-the-job practice	1 2 3 4	1 2 3 4	L
18. Failure to follow through and commit to action	1 2 3 4	1 2 3 4	B
19. Faulty assumptions that lead to inaccurate or unproductive outcomes	1 2 3 4	1 2 3 4	C
20. Greater challenges than available energy/ resources to meet them	1 2 3 4	1 2 3 4	D
21. Inability to change mental models that drive patterns of ineffective behaviors	1 2 3 4	1 2 3 4	C
22. Inability to let go of past ways of thinking or acting	1 2 3 4	1 2 3 4	D
23. Inability to successfully cope with or bounce back from adversity	1 2 3 4	1 2 3 4	D
24. Ineffective decision-making processes	1 2 3 4	1 2 3 4	C
25. Ineffective patterns and styles of communication	1 2 3 4	1 2 3 4	B
26. Inflexible expectations that do not encourage innovation or accept mistakes	1 2 3 4	1 2 3 4	OC
27. Limited expectations about what is possible leading to limited results	1 2 3 4	1 2 3 4	C

Continued

Table A2.1   Continued

Description of Learning & Performance Barriers	Frequency	Impact	(Mapping)
28. Seeing only what reinforces one's existing beliefs	1 2 3 4	1 2 3 4	D
29. Insufficient extrinsic motivation (such as compensation, recognition, other incentives)	1 2 3 4	1 2 3 4	M
30. Insufficient intrinsic motivation to learn and change	1 2 3 4	1 2 3 4	M
31. Organizational functions are separated making communication/collaboration hard	1 2 3 4	1 2 3 4	OSC
32. Pressure to think and act in the same way, resulting in groupthink	1 2 3 4	1 2 3 4	OC
33. Priorities, resources, and people are not aligned	1 2 3 4	1 2 3 4	OSC
34. Setting low expectations to avoid failure and preserve a sense of competence	1 2 3 4	1 2 3 4	D
35. Settling for known solutions that have worked in the past	1 2 3 4	1 2 3 4	L
36. Suppressing failures and ignoring mistakes	1 2 3 4	1 2 3 4	L
37. The presence of unresolved conflict that reduces communication/collaboration	1 2 3 4	1 2 3 4	B
38. Too many changes over a short period of time leading to fatigue and resistance	1 2 3 4	1 2 3 4	B
39. Too much complacency and not enough urgency to make necessary change	1 2 3 4	1 2 3 4	D
40. Treating all goals and outcomes the same and missing critical priorities	1 2 3 4	1 2 3 4	B

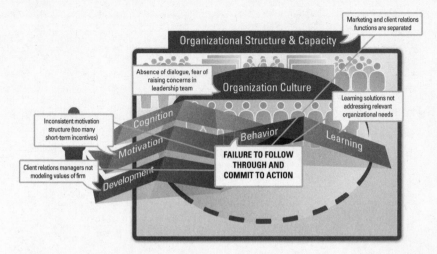

Figure A2.2   Example of Mapping Barriers from the BLPA

"ecosystem view" of the most prominent barriers identified through the assessment. The image in Figure A2.2 provides an example of plotting the results of a BLPA on the conceptual framework. In this case, a team of four colleagues was able to observe the interconnectedness and predictive relationships between their learning and performance issues.

In the image, each box represents a different vantage point, or unique perspective, concerning the specific barrier(s) to workplace learning and performance they experienced. The only barriers that were mapped were those that scored a combined *frequency/impact* score of six or more. By using the assessment tool it allowed the individual members of the team to discover their own perspectives on the shared issues of the team and it gave them an objective language to openly discuss them without finger pointing or personalizing the nature of the challenges. Once this integrated picture emerged for the team, the Nav-Map making process was available to seek specific resolution of the core barriers in a comprehensive manner.

Appendix 3

THE STORY AND SCIENCE BEHIND THE HIDDEN CURRICULUM OF WORK

BEYOND THE JOB DESCRIPTION IS the culmination of more than a decade of research and practice. The cornerstone of this work is the insight that there is a *hidden curriculum of work,* which includes a variety of often unseen challenges that threaten on-going learning and performance for organizations, teams, and their leaders. This is the story of how the effort to define and expose the hidden curriculum of work resulted in the publication of this book.[1]

After working in professional roles as a mediator, facilitator, executive coach, organization development consultant, and internally facing executive for human resources, leadership, and organization development functions, I became increasingly frustrated by the lack of a comprehensive model that could identify and resolve the everyday performance challenges my clients called me in to help "fix." From a practical standpoint, I saw my clients from multiple industries facing the same kinds of recurring problems. From breakdowns in communication to loss of trust and ineffective responses to change, these problems were often felt in the form of presenting headaches and challenges, while the underlying issues remained hidden and left to fester.

Rather than off-the-shelf solutions that met some of the issues, but failed to get to the true root causes of the breakdowns, I needed a framework and set of tools that I could share with individuals and teams that would help them connect-the-dots and identify the intertwined, systemic barriers they experienced. And, I wanted them to be able to continue the learning and performance gains on their own after the consulting and coaching engagements ended. Seeing no available tools and resources that could reliably assist with the identification and resolution of barriers, I channeled my frustrations into academic research that resulted in a PhD for me and what is now the set of resources I refer to as *tools for navigating the hidden curriculum of work.*

THE GROUNDBREAKING STUDY

The science behind the hidden curriculum of work emerged in my doctoral research study, which included the largest literature review of its kind. After completing the literature review, I aggregated a vast inventory of barriers to workplace learning and performance. For organizational purposes, I created a list of a priori categories as a way to initially categorize the identified barriers. This data set represented more than 200 of the most common barriers to learning and performance that were identified and categorized from multiple domains of research and practice, including adult learning and development, management, organizational behavior, developmental psychology (also known as human development), educational psychology, and more.

Drawing on this inventory of issues, the next phase involved the creation of a conceptual framework to link these interconnected barriers. The methodology used for this was the Q-Method, which is a hybrid qualitative-quantitative research method that provides a structured means to explore a given topic of concern by allowing patterns of subjective meaning to emerge from participants' thoughts, beliefs, and perspectives. For the study I developed a Q-Sort assessment tool that was used to explore a wide range of individual experiences with the phenomenon of barriers to workplace learning and performance. (This tool eventually became the BLPA.) Overall, the process validated the most common barriers and provided a new vocabulary to begin mapping what I named "the hidden curriculum of work."

The participants in the study were all experienced professionals from fields such as conflict resolution, management consulting, leadership development, and executive coaching. In addition to substantive interviews about their real-world experience identifying and addressing issues related to learning and performance, the participants sorted the 62 Q-Statements in a way that revealed connections between barriers with regards to impact and frequency of experience. Data gathered during these interviews and Q-Sort activities was subsequently used to refine the conceptual framework and draw conclusions regarding the nature of the phenomenon.

The results of my research confirmed seven categories or dimensions of barriers that sufficiently captured the range of experience with learning and performance gaps. Across these seven dimensions there are distinct barriers that sufficiently explain the most prominent experiences with barriers to workplace learning and performance. In an effort to summarize these results, brief description of each dimension and three exemplary barriers are presented in Tables A3.1–A3.7.

After completing the analysis of these dimensions in light of the remaining research data, I developed a model that presents a more accurate framework to understand barriers to workplace learning and performance. The revised and expanded framework, presented below in Figure A3.1, is based on the sequential and influential relationships identified among the various dimensions. Within the image, the relationships and influences among each of the

Table A3.1 Organizational Structure and Capacity Barriers

DIMENSION #1	ORGANIZATIONAL STRUCTURE & CAPACITY BARRIERS	
DESCRIPTION	DEFINING CHARACTERISTICS	EXAMPLE BARRIERS
Organizational Structure and Capacity Barriers refer to the strategic and operational levers and drivers inherent in the organizational system, including specific limitations related to the organization's structure and capacity, such as the organization's central values and practices concerning learning, its access to and allocation of resources, and its ability to innovate.	• The organization's responsiveness to internal and external changes; • Engagement levels of the workforce; • The integration of human capital; and • The ability to identify and execute on internal learning and performance needs.	Inability or unwillingness to adapt to fast changing, complex, or uncertain conditions. Organizational functions are separated, making communication, decision making and transfer of learning unsuccessful. Overly formal and bureaucratic or excessively informal and decentralized organizational structures that do not support learning and performance initiatives.

Table A3.2 Organization Culture Barriers

DIMENSION #2	ORGANIZATION CULTURE BARRIERS	
DESCRIPTION	DEFINING CHARACTERISTICS	EXAMPLE BARRIERS
Organization Culture Barriers reference a wide variety of cultural facets that emerge within the life span of the organization.	• The collective attitudes and established norms; • The written and unwritten rules that influence behavior; • The inclusiveness of diversity; and • The tolerance toward risk and innovation.	Absence of dialogue and limited expression of diverse viewpoints. An organizational culture that enables polarized views and split alliances. Too many changes over a short period of time, leading to fatigue and resistance to essential changes.

Table A3.3 Cognition Barriers

DIMENSION #3	COGNITION BARRIERS	
DESCRIPTION	DEFINING CHARACTERISTICS	EXAMPLE BARRIERS
Cognition Barriers are concerned with a variety of inner thinking and processing dynamics.	• The individuals' perceptual processes; • Problem-solving abilities and reasoning abilities; • The mental models and conceptual frameworks that influence their attitudes, decisions; and • Behaviors, as well as their beliefs about the organization.	Faulty assumptions that lead to inaccurate or unproductive outcomes. Inability to consistently identify, synthesize, conceptualize, and integrate ambiguous, contradictory, or shifting information. Inability to let go of past ways of thinking or acting.

Table A3.4 Motivation Barriers

DIMENSION #4	MOTIVATION BARRIERS	
DESCRIPTION	**DEFINING CHARACTERISTICS**	**EXAMPLE BARRIERS**
Motivation Barriers refer to the barriers that affect how and why a person learns at a given level.	• Intrinsic and extrinsic forms of individual motivation; • Perspectives or opinions held toward a particular person or issue; • Emotional states or moods such as anxiety, complacency, urgency, indifference, or excitement; and • Self-labels concerning identity.	Minimal intrinsic motivation to learn and change. Negative, cynical, indifferent, or resistant attitude toward learning and performance activities. Too much complacency and not enough urgency to make necessary change.

Table A3.5 Development Barriers

DIMENSION #5	DEVELOPMENT BARRIERS	
DESCRIPTION	**DEFINING CHARACTERISTICS**	**EXAMPLE BARRIERS**
Development Barriers refer to issues related to the current state and capacity for transitioning through stages of developing.	• Individual levels of emotional intelligence; • Capacity for advanced conceptual understanding; • Critical thinking, reflection, and problem-solving capability and the ability to utilize language for conceptualizing and communicating complex ideas; and • Knowledge and articulation of personal values.	Inability to successfully cope with or bounce back from adversity. Lack of reflection and learning from past successes and failures. Poor self-awareness and self-management.

Table A3.6 Behavior Barriers

DIMENSION #6	BEHAVIOR BARRIERS	
DESCRIPTION	DEFINING CHARACTERISTICS	EXAMPLE BARRIERS
Behavior Barriers include myriad uses of discretionary energy that individuals put toward organizational tasks and activities through the course of their work. Specifically, behavioral barriers comprise larger categories of actions.	• Communication; • Problem solving; • Decision making; and • Time and priority management.	The presence of unresolved conflict that reduces effective communication and collaboration. Suppressing failures and ignoring mistakes. Attempting to implement new behaviors and practices without changing the system that keeps old behaviors in place.

Table A3.7 Learning Barriers

DIMENSION #7	LEARNING BARRIERS	
DESCRIPTION	DEFINING CHARACTERISTICS	EXAMPLE BARRIERS
Learning Barriers include a range of individual, team, and organization-wide factors that impact the learning process in some way.	• Accountability for learning outcomes; • Alignment between learning objectives and organizational needs; • Buy-in and investment of the learner; and • The appropriateness of the timing and setting of learning.	Treating all goals and outcomes the same thus diverting energy and attention from the most critical priorities. Greater challenges and demands than available energy and resources to address them. Learning objectives and activities that address only symptoms but not underlying causes of problems.

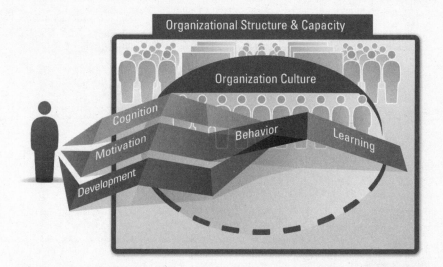

Figure A3.1 Conceptual Framework of Barriers to Workplace Learning and Performance

seven dimensions are indicated by the specific orientation and placement of each component.

Within the framework you can see the individual and collective come together. The micro experiences of individuals merge with the macro experiences of the team and larger organization. Individual roles, choices, and decisions impact the outer levels of culture and organizational system. Likewise, the organization itself is a generative environment that informs and influences individuals and teams based on its parameters. The spatial relationship among these seven dimensions offers a meaningful way to conceptualize the myriad examples of barriers that they represent. Specifically, the organization structure and capacity barriers act as an all-encompassing boundary that sets the physical parameters for all of the others. The inner macro-level dimension—organization culture barriers—is directly influenced by the organization structure and capacity while it also influences all of the other dimensions of barriers.

The three dimensions on the left—cognitive, motivation, and developmental barriers—exist both inside and outside of the boundaries of the organization. This placement represents the preexisting experiences that individuals contribute to their organizational system. Inside the culture of the organization, these three categories directionally influence behavior barriers which, in turn, directly influence learning barriers. The dimension of learning barriers is intentionally spaced to overlap the macro dimensions of cultural and structural

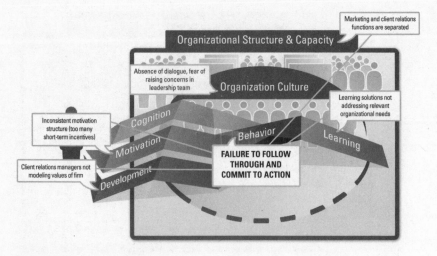

Figure A3.2   Example of a Team's Barriers Plotted in the Framework

barriers. This arrangement suggests that learning both impacts and is impacted by these two macro dimensions.

Utilizing this systemic framework as point of reference can provide a clearer lens through which barriers to workplace learning and performance can be observed and understood within a larger context of other related barriers. Once we see and learn from the relationships between and among barriers, we understand what is possible as it relates to intervention. Figure A3.2 includes an example of a team that assessed their core barriers and subsequently plotted them within the framework. Even without knowing any of the specific background of the team's challenges, seeing barriers within the relevant dimensions already facilitates the path toward resolution:

LIMITS IN THE RESEARCH

It should be noted that I limited my research of barriers in several specific ways. In essence, my investigation of barriers to workplace learning and performance did not include any of the following examples of external barriers: Deficits or significant weakness in cognitive functioning (e.g., a learning disability); Barriers stemming from general mental health issues and diagnosed or undiagnosed psychoses; Capability gaps due to physical limitations or disabilities, decrements of aging, or injuries; and Physical (e.g., the space is too small, time is too short) and institutional barriers (racism, social inequality, etc.), which may indeed adversely impact learning and performance but were not relevant to the research study.

FROM RESEARCH, TO PRACTICE, TO THE BOOK

In the months and years following the initial study, I designed, tested, and refined the resources, tools, and guided coaching methods that rest on the foundation of the research. The original Q-Method Study was converted to the BLPA, which is included in Appendix 2. And the conceptual framework of barriers ultimately resulted in the Nav-Map process, which draws on the concept of Constellations of Barriers, Varying Perspectives of Barriers (VPB), and Trip-Wire Patterns that sustain the effects of barriers.

Overall, the use of these tools and practices with leaders and their teams has resulted in a range of versatile methods for teaching people to accelerate their own learning and performance through a comprehensive, systemic approach to exploring and navigating the hidden curriculum of work. The results have demonstrated the effectiveness of the tools and the potential to create lasting change.

As it relates to creating change in behavior and performance, all of the associated tools and methods of *Beyond the Job Description* reflect a baseline of *knowledge for action*.[2] This means that one of the fundamental aims of this work is to contribute useful knowledge that can be used to solve people's pressing problems at work in such a way that increases individual, team, and organizational learning and performance.[3] To deliver on this aim, the book rests on integrated theories of change and action.

A *theory of change* identifies the various processes through which a given change is expected to occur. A *theory of action* maps out the specific ways in which that theory of change, including the individual and organizational roles with respect to achieving that change, will occur. Both of these are explained here, beginning first with the *theory of action* that is embedded within *Beyond the Job Description*:

- The widely accepted Standard Model of Work (SMW) suggests that work is broadly understood and communicated to employees via their job descriptions for the positions they were hired to fill;
- This superficial interpretation of work leads to three common misperceptions, including:
  1. A person's job description is the primary source for information and direction about what they should do to perform effectively;
  2. The tasks and activities it reflects represent an accurate set of indicators about the most important success factors for the role; and

3. If a person fulfills the duties outlined on their job description consistently they will succeed at work in the short and long term.

- The changing nature of work, including the increasing demands on employees to stay vital, improve their own learning and development, and remain competitive in the job market challenges these beliefs and the relevance of the SMW;

- The new reality of work requires a different perspective for employees to succeed, including an understanding that:

  1. You were hired to fill a job, but it also came with a second "job-within-the-job" that nobody told you about;

  2. These two jobs, combined with the need to stay ahead of the change curve and add increasing value to your organization, represent your hidden curriculum of work;

  3. Everyone confronts their own hidden curriculum of work and nobody is immune from its challenges and demands; and

  4. The people who succeed in their careers over the long-term will be those who develop a specific set of skills to reveal their hidden challenges of work and transform them into opportunities to boost their learning and performance and add increasing value to their organizations beyond their job descriptions.

With this theory of action as a foundation, the theory of change reflected in *Breakthrough Performance* involves a set of assumptions and beliefs that have been confirmed through research, practice, and careful observation in the workplace. It includes an inherent assumption that *identifying and potentially reducing barriers may directly or indirectly improve the probability of successful workplace learning and performance*. The primary foundation of this assumption comes from Kurt Lewin, the father of organization development, and his groundbreaking ideas on change management described as "force-field analysis."

In force-field analysis, one can either reduce the strength of the forces opposing a desired change (e.g. barriers), or can increase the forces driving the change. However, rather than framing the potential for change as an "either/or" (i.e., either reduce the roadblocks, or increase the resources and supports) *Beyond the Job Description* offers a "both/and" by simultaneously moving in both of these directions. The R-I-T-E Model resolves barriers (reduces challenges) while also enhancing the capacity for on-going learning and performance (increasing resources). Moving beyond the concept of force-field analysis, several additional factors reflected in this theory of change include the following:

1. In the course of every day work-life, everyone experiences barriers to their learning and performance (they may refer to them with different names and experience different effects depending on their role, tenure, perspective, and power in the workplace);

2. Certain barriers to workplace learning and performance predictably surface at various stages of organizational life (i.e., when a person is new to an organization or work team, when an individual has been entrenched in workplace culture for a long period of time etc.);

3. What is perceived as a "barrier" by one person may actually be an "opportunity" to another person depending upon one's experience. Therefore, at a certain level, the very notion of barriers to workplace learning and performance is socially constructed and deeply subjective; and

4. Reducing core barriers and associated gaps leads to improved learning and performance.

Taken together, the related theory of change and theory of action described above complete the foundational assumptions of *Beyond the Job Description*. Despite the rich foundation of research and practice, the reality is that the story and science behind the hidden curriculum of work is still being written and will evolve along with the changing nature of work and on-going challenges that individuals, leaders, and their teams must confront.

Appendix 4

ADDITIONAL RESOURCES TO NAVIGATE THE HIDDEN CURRICULUM OF WORK

THE NAV-ROOM IS AN online source for information and resources to help people find their "extra" and stay competitive at work. The interactive blog and website deliver high-impact tools for learning and performance. Visit the www.beyondthejobdescription.com to discover insights and tools, including:

- **Nav-Coaching**

  1:1 Coaching to Help Individuals Navigate Their Hidden Curriculum of Work and Get Future-Proofed

- **Nav-Academy**

  On-Demand Programs to Help Individuals Navigate Their Hidden Curriculum of Work and Get Future-Proofed

- **Nav-Maps**

  On-Demand Requests for Customized Nav-Maps to Resolve Specific Individual or Team Barriers

- **Nav-Programs**

  On-Site One-Day and Two-Day Programs to Help Organizations and Their Leaders Identify the Hidden Curriculum of Work and Create Future-Proof Leaders and Teams

- **Nav-Consulting**

  Customized Consulting for Organizations Using the Wisdom, Tools, and Conceptual Frameworks of the Hidden Curriculum of Work

- **BLPA to Identify Core Barriers**

  Order the BLPA to Identify Individual/Team Core Barriers

ABOUT THE AUTHOR

JESSE SOSTRIN IS A SOUGHT-AFTER consultant and speaker working at the intersection of individual and organizational success. The results of his innovative research and practice on the *hidden challenges of work* have helped countless organizations and their leaders navigate a unique path to success through the complex changes of our time.

As the president of Sostrin Consulting, he spearheads solution-driven consulting engagements for a wide range of companies, including Fortune 500 clients. As an executive coach, he is an expert at diagnosing workplace problems and identifying solutions that align with company goals and professional development priorities. As a keynote speaker, his signature blend of inspirational and results-oriented thought leadership translates to highly interactive, skill focused programs that challenge leaders to create world-class cultures within their organizations.

His recent book *Re-Making Communication at Work* turned the conventional wisdom about "what works with workplace communication" upside down and established his place in the next generation of influential writers and thinkers, challenging everything we thought we knew about success at work.

NOTES

INTRODUCTION

1. Nikki Blacksmith and Jim Harter, "Majority of American Workers Not Engaged in Their Jobs," *Gallup Wellbeing*, October 28, 2011, http://www.gallup.com/poll /150383/majority-american-workers-not-engaged-jobs.aspx (accessed on April 18, 2013).
2. The phrase "hidden curriculum of work" is a trademark of Jesse Sostrin. For formatting reasons, the phrase will be referred to throughout the book as "the hidden curriculum of work."

1   THE MYTH OF YOUR WORKING LIFE

1. Kingsley Davis, *Human Society* (New York: Macmillan, 1942).
2. The phrase *hidden curriculum* was first coined by Philip Jackson in 1968, and then elaborated upon by Benson Snyder in 1970. Both explored the concept within the realm of education and youth development. I have applied a new, expanded definition of the term to the world of work.
3. Howard McClusky, "Education for Aging: The Scope of the Field and Perspectives for the Future," in Learning *for Aging*, ed. Stanley Grabowski and Dean Mason (Washington, DC: Adult Education Association of the USA, 1974), 324–355.
4. Wendell Berry, "Solving for Pattern,"in *The Gift of Good Land: Further Essays Cultural & Agricultural* (North Point Press, 1981), chap. 9. Originally published in the Rodale Press periodical *The New Farm*.
5. Nikki Blacksmith and Jim Harter, "Majority of American Workers Not Engaged in Their Jobs," *Gallup Wellbeing*, October 28, 2011, http://www.gallup.com/poll /150383/majority-american-workers-not-engaged-jobs.aspx (accessed on April 18, 2013).
6. "The High Cost of Disengaged Employees," Q & A with Curt Coffman, http:// businessjournal.gallup.com/content/247/the-high-cost-of-disengaged-employees .aspx (accessed on January 21, 2013).

7. "What Drives Employee Engagement and Why It Matters" from Dale Carnegie Training http://www.dalecarnegie.com/imap/white_papers/employee_engagement_white_paper/ (accessed on January 21, 2013).

8. An article called "Great Britain's Workforce Lacks Inspiration," by Peter Flade, appeared in the online *Gallup Business Journal*. More than 80 percent of British workers lack any real commitment to their jobs, and a quarter of those are "actively disengaged," or truly disaffected with their workplaces. These are among the troubling findings of The Gallup Organization's Employee Engagement Index survey, which examines employee engagement levels in several countries, including Great Britain. See http://businessjournal.gallup.com/content/9847/great-britains-workforce-lacks-inspiration.aspx (accessed on December 21, 2012).

9. Kevin Ford and James Osterhaus, *The Thing in the Bushes: Turning Organizational Blind Spots into Competitive Advantage* (Colorado Springs, CO: Pinon Press, 2001).

2   RETHINKING THE WAY WE WORK

1. Gary Stern, "Company Training Programs: What Are They Really Worth?" *Fortune*, May 27, 2011, http://management.fortune.cnn.com/2011/05/27/company-training-programs-what-are-they-really-worth/ (accessed on January 30, 2013).

3   AVERAGE IS OVER

1. Thomas Friedman, *The World Is Flat: A Brief History of the 21st Century* (New York: Farrar, Straus and Giroux, 2005).

2. According to the Bureau of Labor Statistics, the average worker currently holds ten different jobs before age 40, and this number is projected to grow. Forrester Research predicts that today's youngest workers will hold 12–15 jobs in their lifetime. See http://www.experience.com/alumnus/article?channel_id=career_management&source_page=additional_articles&article_id=article_1247505066959 (accessed on January 30, 2013)

3. Doug Hall, *Careers in Organizations* (Glenview, IL: Goodyear Publishing, 1976) and Ann Howard, *The Changing Nature of Work* (San Francisco: Jossey-Bass, 1995).

4. Peter Vaill, *Learning as a Way of Being* (San Francisco, CA: Jossey-Bass, 1996), 43.

5. Peter Vaill, *Learning as a Way of Being* (San Francisco, CA: Jossey-Bass, 1996), 43.

6. Friedman, *The World Is Flat*.

7. Thomas Friedman, "Average Is Over," *New York Times,* January 24, 2012, http://www.nytimes.com/2012/01/25/opinion/friedman-average-is-over.html?_r=1 (accessed on February 21, 2013).

8. Robert Kegan, *In over Our Heads: The Mental Demands Of Modern Life* (Cambridge, MA: Harvard University Press, 1994).

9. Sunny Lurie, "Employee Learning in Dynamic Work Settings: An Exploration of Adult Learning in Business Organizations," *Fielding Graduate University Dissertation Database*, 2000). Retrieved April 15, 2008 from Fielding Dissertation and Theses Database.

10. Eleni Stavrou-Costea, "The Challenges of Human Resource Management towards Organizational Effectiveness: A Comparative Study in Southern EU," *Journal of European Industrial Training* 29 (February 2005): 112–134. Kenneth Zula and Thomas Chermack, "Human Capital Planning: A Review of Literature and Implications for Human Resource Development," *Human Resource Development Review* 6 (2007): 245.

11. Peter Drucker, *Post-Capitalist Society* (New York: HarperCollins, 1993).

12. Daniel Pink, A *Whole New Mind: Moving From the Information Age to the Conceptual Age* (New York: Riverhead Books, 2005).

13. Tom Peters, *Thriving On Chaos: Handbook for a Managerial Revolution* (London: Macmillan, 1987).

5   SEEING YOUR "JOB-WITHIN-THE-JOB"

1. Information about ordering the full BLPA is included in appendix 4.

2. David Cooperrider, Diana Whitney, and Jacqueline Stavros, *Appreciative Inquiry Handbook* (Bedford Heights, OH: Lakeshore Publishers, 2003).

3. Kurt Lewin, *Field Theory and Social Science* (New York: Harper, 1951).

6   TRANSFORMING HIDDEN CHALLENGES WITH "NAV-MAPS"

1. Steven Few, *Now You See It: Simple Visualization Techniques for Quantitative Analysis* (Oakland, CA: Analytics Press, 2009), 53.

7   SUCCESS STORIES FROM THE HIDDEN SIDE OF WORK

1. An early version of this case example was described in Jesse Sostrin, "Transforming Barriers to Learning and Performance," *OD Practitioner* 43, no. 2 (Spring 2011): 14–21.

2. Jerry Gilley and Ann Maycunich, *Beyond the Learning Organization* (New York: Perseus Books, 2000).

9   QUANTIFY YOUR INVESTMENT

1. Thomas Kayser, *Mining Group Gold: How to Cash in on the Collaborative Brain Power of a Group* (El Segundo, CA: Serif Publishing, 1990).

2. Nicholas Romano and Jay Nunamaker, *Meeting Analysis: Findings from Research and Practice,* Proceedings of the 34th Hawaii International Conference on System

Sciences, September, 2001, http://www.okstate.edu/ceat/msetm/courses/etm5221 /Week%201%20Challenges/Meeting%20Analysis%20Findings%20from%20 Research%20and%20Practice.pdf (accessed on February 7, 2013).

10   THE ANSWER TO OVERWORKED AND DISENGAGED

1. Nikki Blacksmith and Jim Harter, "Majority of American Workers Not Engaged in Their Jobs," *Gallup Wellbeing*, October 28, 2011, http://www.gallup.com/poll /150383/majority-american-workers-not-engaged-jobs.aspx (accessed on April 18, 2013).

2. "What Drives Employee Engagement and Why It Matters," from Dale Carnegie Training, http://www.dalecarnegie.com/imap/white_papers/employee_engagement _white_paper/ (accessed on January 21, 2013).

3. "The High Cost of Disengaged Employees," Q & A with Curt Coffman,: http:// businessjournal.gallup.com/content/247/the-high-cost-of-disengaged-employees .aspx (accessed on January 21, 2013).

4. An earlier version of this set of four common barriers was first described in Jesse Sostrin, *Re-Making Communication at Work* (New York: Palgrave Macmillan, 2013).

5. Alain de Botton, "A Kinder, Gentler Philosophy of Success," http://www.ted.com/ talks/alain_de_botton_a_kinder_gentler_philosophy_of_success.html (accessed on January 7, 2013).

11   CREATE YOUR FUTURE-PROOF PLAN

1. In my book *Re-Making Communication at Work* I provide an extensive knowledge guide to understanding how to intentionally create the patterns of communication and interaction that produce the experiences you seek in the world of work. Jesse Sostrin, *Re-Making Communication at Work* (New York: Palgrave Macmillan, 2013).

12   YOUR DAILY COMPASS FOR SOLO NAVIGATION

1. Confirmation bias (also called confirmatory bias or my side bias) is a tendency of people to favor information that confirms their beliefs. The term "confirmation bias" was coined by the British psychologist Peter Wason. See http://en.wikipedia .org/wiki/Confirmation_bias (accessed on January 30, 2013.)

14   MANAGING TO THE HIDDEN SIDE OF WORK

1. While this may seem counterintuitive, research indicates clearly that engaged employees perform consistently better than disengaged employees. When individuals are

given the opportunity to pursue work that aligns with their own values and aspirations they are naturally more invested in their work, which leads to ownership and follow-through on priorities. Managers who do not acknowledge this dynamic or invest time and energy into understanding their employees' goals for their working lives run the risk of increased disengagement.

15   CULTIVATING FUTURE-PROOF LEADERS AND ORGANIZATIONAL CULTURES

1. This chapter contains several definitions of leadership and organizational culture that I first wrote about in *Re-Making Communication at Work*. The excerpts do not provide the full definition as it relates to the communication perspective; however they are included here to emphasize a more dynamic view of the role leaders play in making culture as the lead architects of patterns of interaction. See Jesse Sostrin, *Re-Making Communication at Work* (New York: Palgrave Macmillan, 2013).

2. Terrence Deal and Allan Kennedy, *Corporate Cultures: The Rites and Rituals of Corporate Life* (Harmondsworth: Penguin Books, 1982).

3. Fredric Jablin, "Organizational Entry, Assimilation, and Exit" in *Handbook of Organizational Communication*, ed. Fredric Jablin, Linda Putnam, K. Roberts, and L.W. Porter (Newbury Park, CA: Sage Publications, 1987), 679–740.

4. Amitai Etzioni, *Modern Organizations* (Englewood Cliffs, NJ: Prentice-Hall, 1964), 1.

5. Daniel Katz and Robert Kahn, *The Social Psychology of Organizations*, 2nd ed. (New York: John Wiley & Sons, 1978), 428.

6. The Great Place to Work Culture Audit, http://www.greatplacetowork.com/ (accessed on January 30, 2013).

7. Chris Argyris, *Knowledge for Action* (San Francisco, CA: Jossey-Bass, 1993): 243.

8. Sidney Rosen and Abraham Tesser, "On Reluctance to Communicate Undesirable Information: The MUM Effect," *Sociometry* 33, no. 3 (September 1970): 253–263.

9. Chris Argyris, *Knowledge for Action* (San Francisco, CA: Jossey-Bass, 1993), 243.

APPENDIX 2   THE 40-STATEMENT BLPA

1. For more information about the science behind the BLPA, refer to Appendix 3: The Story and Science behind the Hidden Curriculum of Work.

APPENDIX 3   THE STORY AND SCIENCE BEHIND THE HIDDEN CURRICULUM OF WORK

1. Several aspects of the story and science behind the hidden curriculum of work have been published in the recent article: Jesse Sostrin, "A Systemic Cause Analysis

Model for Human Performance Technicians," *Performance Improvement Journal* 52, no. 7 (September 2011): 17–23.

2. *Knowledge for Action* was the title of a book by Chris Argyris. In the preface of that book he described two of his lifelong commitments, both of which included efforts to design the research methods that would produce valid, actionable knowledge to help organizations achieve their stated aims. Chris Argyris, *Knowledge for Action* (San Francisco, CA: Jossey-Bass, 1993).

3. The tradition of *Action Research* involves an emphasis on the real world, including the identification of how people consider, design, and implement their actions in difficult situations, as well as practical ways to close the gaps between what people want to have in their experience *and* what they actually get. This starts with analyzing the Espoused Theories we have about work compared to the Theories-In-Use we follow. Espoused Theories reflect what people say they will think and do in a given situation, while the Theories-In-Use represent what they actually do in that situation.

BIBLIOGRAPHY

Berry, Wendell. "Solving for Pattern." In *The Gift of Good Land: Further Essays Cultural & Agricultural*. San Francisco, CA: North Point Press, 1981. Cooperrider, David, Diana Whitney, and Jacqueline Stavros. *Appreciative Inquiry Handbook*. Bedford Heights, OH: Lakeshore Publishers, 2003.

Davis, Kingsley. *Human Society*. New York: Macmillan, 1942.

Deal, Terrence, and Allan Kennedy. *Corporate Cultures: The Rites and Rituals of Corporate Life*. Harmondsworth, UK: Penguin Books, 1982.

Drucker, Peter. *Post-Capitalist Society*. New York: HarperCollins, 1993.

Etzioni, Amitai. *Modern Organizations*. Englewood Cliffs, NJ: Prentice-Hall, 1964.

Few, Steven. *Now You See It: Simple Visualization Techniques for Quantitative Analysis*. Oakland, CA: Analytics Press, 2009.

Ford, Kevin, and James Osterhaus. *The Thing in the Bushes: Turning Organizational Blind Spots into Competitive Advantage*. Colorado Springs, CO: Pinon Press, 2001.

Friedman, Thomas. *The World Is Flat: A Brief History of the 21st Century*. New York: Farrar, Straus and Giroux, 2005.

Gilley, Jerry, and Ann Maycunich. *Beyond the Learning Organization*. New York: Perseus Books, 2000.

Hall, Doug. *Careers in Organizations*. Glenview, IL: Goodyear Publishing, 1976.

Howard, Ann, *The Changing Nature of Work*. San Francisco, CA: Jossey-Bass, 1995.

Jablin, Fredric. "Organizational Entry, Assimilation, and Exit." In *Handbook of Organizational Communication*, edited by Fredric Jablin, Linda Putnam, K. Roberts, and L.W. Porter, 679–740. Newbury Park, CA: Sage Publications, 1987.

Katz, Daniel, and Robert Kahn. *The Social Psychology of Organizations*. New York: John Wiley & Sons, 1978.

Kayser, Thomas. *Mining Group Gold: How to Cash in on the Collaborative Brain Power of A Group*. El Segundo: Serif Publishing, 1990.

Kegan, Robert. *In over Our Heads: The Mental Demands Of Modern Life*. Cambridge, MA: Harvard University Press, 1994.

Lewin, Kurt. *Field Theory and Social Science*. New York: Harper, 1951.

McClusky, Howard. "Education For Aging: The Scope of the Field and Perspectives for the Future." In *Learning for Aging*, edited by Stanley Grabowski and Dean Mason, 324–355. Washington, DC: Adult Education Association of the USA, 1974.

Peters, Tom. *Thriving on Chaos: Handbook for a Managerial Revolution*. New York: Alfred A. Knopf, 1987.

Pink, Daniel. A *Whole New Mind: Moving from the Information Age to the Conceptual Age*. New York: Riverhead Books, 2005.

Sostrin, Jesse. *Re-Making Communication at Work*. New York: Palgrave Macmillan, 2013.

Vaill, Peter. *Learning As a Way of Being*. San Francisco, CA: Jossey-Bass, 1996.

INDEX